YOUR FAMILY

A Love & Maintenance Manual for People with Parents & Other Relatives

A HIS Reader

Jim Conway, Walter Trobisch & Others

InterVarsity Press
Downers Grove
Illinois 60515

InterVarsity Press is the book-publishing division of Inter-Varsity Christian Fellowship, a student movement active on campus at hundreds of universities, colleges and schools of nursing. For information about local and regional activities, write IVCF, 233 Langdon St., Madison, WI 53703.

Distributed in Canada through InterVarsity Press, 1875 Leslie St., Unit 10, Don Mills, Ontario M3B 2M5, Canada.

ISBN 0-87784-370-8

Printed in the United States of America

Library of Congress Cataloging in Publication Data

Main entry under title:

Your family.

Bibliography: p.

1. Family—Religious life—Addresses, essays, lectures. I. Conway, Jim. II. His.

BV4526.2.Y68 248.4 81-20809

ISBN 0-87784-370-8 AACR2

17 16 15 14 13 12 11 10 9 8 7 6 5 4 3 2 1

95 94 93 92 91 90 89 88 87 86 85 84 83 82

Part 3: Coping with Problems

Part 4: Growing Up

Foreword

Most of us have families. We need them more than we admit. They need us more than we realize.

Coping with our present family relationships and planning for or worrying about future ones may be the biggest of all the problems we wrestle with in life. So we can use all the help we can get, right?

The sixteen chapters of this book are like case studies—written by people who are also wrestling—on how God wants us, and enables us, to live in our families. I'm glad these eighteen people were willing to open up and share their insights in articles which first appeared in HIS magazine. The Scriptures put it this way: " . . . in an abundance of counselors there is safety" (Prov 11:14).

Unless your family is perfect (in which case please write and tell us how you achieved *that*) you'll find a lot of biblical wisdom and practical help here.

Linda Doll, Editor, HIS magazine

Part 1
Home Is Where the Heart Is

Understanding Your Parents

by Jim Conway

1

"I don't understand my parents. It's bothering me, because I used to look up to them, but now they seem so unstable. We get into conflicts about almost everything—the way I spend my money, the Christian friends that I associate with, where I'm going to live this summer. It seems we're always in a conflict about religion.

"Sometimes it's so bad that I never want to go home again. Vacations are the worst time. I keep thinking, 'How will I ever make it through?' "

Quite often students and others talk to me about the deep depression and conflicts which their parents are in. Or they tell me that their parents seem to have no meaning or direction in their lives. Their parents seem to be angry about everything and unstable in many decisions.

Crisis Can Be Normal In recent years, people have become aware that there are some normal developmental crises which take place in adults during the midyears. Your mom may be experiencing a great deal of stress in her mid to late thirties and again in her late forties. Your dad may begin to experience a stress of crisis proportion during his forties.

The parents of most college-age young people are in this critical age zone of thirty-five to fifty. You may feel that the family stress is your fault, when in fact it may have little or nothing to do with you. It may have everything to do with the time in life of your parents. This is an era of life when they are struggling with some issues they haven't thought about for a number of years. (A number of books have been published which talk about the normal developmental crises of the midlife era. Perhaps the best and most readable among secular books is Gail Sheehy's book *Passages,* which describes each of the developmental stress areas of life from the twenties to retirement.)

Your parents might be described as restless, introspective, rather moody, and sometimes melancholy. Your dad or mom may be having trouble at work, feeling that it is not important. They may even wonder why they are working at their jobs. If you talk with your parents about their life, they may say that it is awful, boring, dull, or depressing—without being able to say exactly why. One of them might be looking for greener pastures, daydreaming about running away with someone who will really appreciate them. In other words, their marriage might also be in real trouble.

The problem is that parents do need help, but they probably won't accept it, especially from someone your age. The parents have thought of themselves as the leaders of the family, the ones who have everything all put together, and they have looked at their children as the learners who didn't have their heads screwed on quite right.

It may be now, however, that the situation is reversed, especially if the son or daughter has come to Christ and has settled some of the major issues of life. It may really be that he or she is stronger than the parent at this time, but the self-image of the parent makes it difficult to allow the child to help. Therefore, any help you offer must come in very tactful ways.

How to Help 1. *Appreciate your parents.* Appreciation is a subtle but genuine way of strengthening your parents' self-image. Tell them face to face, looking right in their eyes, that you are grateful for them. List specific things—nothing phony —for which you are truly thankful. The more specific and direct, the better. This verbal appreciation should come as a continual flow—in letters, phone calls, and any time when you are physically together.

Appreciation can also be expressed by touching your parents. When you walk past your dad as he is sitting, reading the paper or watching TV, reach out and give his shoulder a squeeze. As your mom works in the kitchen, give her a couple of love pats on the back. If you pray at meals, reach out and hold each other's hands. Take the opportunity to throw your arms around them and give them a good hug when you first greet them or when you're leaving, going to bed, or excited about something.

You may come from a family where "we just don't show emotion like that. They'll think I've flipped." Chances are great they won't. It may open up your relationship in ways you never suspected.

2. *Pray.* Do you believe that God is all-powerful? Do you believe that he answers prayer? Do you believe that he is concerned for your parents? Then pray for them to be strengthened and blessed by God. Do I hear you say that I don't know *your* parents? Are you telling me that the God who created heaven and earth and who made the intricate human personality is absolutely baffled by your stubborn parents? I don't believe it!

Jesus repeatedly showed us God's miraculous power. Begin to draw on that power and believe that he can help your parents. And enlist your friends to pray with you for your parents.

3. *Do little favors for your parents.* Increase the number

of your letters and phone calls. When you are home, volunteer to do things which you may not have done before. Send them a card, telling them that you appreciate them, and enclose a fifteen-dollar check so that the two of them can go out to dinner.

One day as I went into my office and sat down to start working, I noticed that on one of my scratch pads one of my daughters had written, "I love you, Dad," and signed her name. That warmed my heart! Send your dad a note at his office. Have the florist deliver a single flower to your mom.

4. *Strengthen the stronger parent.* If one of your parents is going through a tremendous crisis, he or she needs your help, but the other parent is having to carry a giant load too. Encourage the one who is carrying the big load. Let him or her know you understand and that you're praying. Have coffee together, opening opportunities to share burdens with you. Many times parents are reluctant to share their struggles with other people (though they long to), because everyone believes that when you become an adult your head ought to be together.

5. *Encourage your parents' friends to help.* Perhaps you know a strong Christian couple or individual who has been close to your parents and who could help. Go to these people and ask them to help you meet the needs of your parents. If you can enlist several people to help from the neighborhood, the church, work, their small Bible study group, or other social contacts, you will then broaden the base of encouragement for your parents.

6. *Encourage your parents to plan short breaks or vacations.* Help them get past their guilt feelings about spending money or about taking off from work in order to go on a short break. Tell them you'll watch the house, the dog, and grandma.

7. *Share with them verses from the Bible that are helping you as you face the major questions of life.* It may surprise you, but your parents are probably at a time when they are again wrestling with questions such as "Who am I? What do I want to do with my life? What are my values?" As God helps you answer

your questions, share this with your parents.

Don't start preaching at them but in letters or over the phone or when you're at home, simply say, "Hey, I found this neat verse in the Bible," or "I've been reading a book that has reminded me of God's care and love for me." Lovingly share with them how God is changing you so that you look at life, God, other people, and your parents differently.

The struggles which your parents are going through will, perhaps, provide an opportunity for you to become their peer, no longer dependent on them to only minister to you. Now you can move into an interdependent relationship where you minister to them as well.

Jim Conway, former pastor at Twin City Bible Church, Urbana, Illinois, is director of the Doctor of Ministry program at Talbot Theological Seminary in La Mirada, California. This article and chapter fifteen originally appeared in the popular HIS feature "Free to Be."

The Real Story behind the Fifth

by John W. Howe

2

Do you have trouble with your parents? If you do, don't write off the help God offers you. Look at Exodus 20:12. "Honor your father and mother, that your days may be long in the land which the LORD your God gives you."

Sound old-fashioned? Irrelevant? Like the same old worn-out advice? I don't think so. Stop and take a closer look at what God is *really* saying here.

For Adults First, this commandment is not directed toward small children. It is directed toward adults, or rather toward children who have grown up.

In the society to which this commandment was given, the father was king. His word was law; there was no higher court of appeal. He could be arbitrary, selfish, or perverse; he could even sell his family into slavery to pay off a debt.

But once a man married and left his father and mother, his relationship to them changed completely. Now *he* was king and they, all too often, were forgotten and abandoned. When the aged could no longer pull their own weight economically, they were cast out of society to die by exposure or to be killed by wild beasts. This was the societal norm.

But then came the commandment: Honor your parents when they have long since lost their financial usefulness. And civilization took a mighty leap forward.

So the fifth commandment is not something that we grow out of, but something we grow into. It is a responsibility we can assume only when we are no longer under obligation to our parents. It is assumed voluntarily. It is not demanded of us.

Honor and Obedience Second, the commandment doesn't talk about obedience, it talks about honor. Anybody who thinks that honor and obedience are the same either has no backbone or knows nothing of conscience. The apostle Peter who wrote "Honor the emperor" also said, "We ought rather to obey God than men." You can honor those you disobey for conscience's sake. And you can dishonor those you obey. We are called to honor, not necessarily to obey.

A little child should, of course, obey his parents. If he doesn't, he's punished. This has little to do with honoring his parents. Perhaps only as the child outgrows the requirements of obedience can he have the opportunity of honoring.

To "honor," according to the Random House Dictionary, is to "regard with high public esteem." Parents who quote the fifth commandment to their children in an effort to get them to knuckle under to their demands have missed the point entirely. They may be able to create a disrespectful subservience, but that's the opposite of the commandment. Honoring is something I do freely, because I want to. It can't be demanded of me. It is something I do publicly and joyfully, not something I do shamefully while gritting my teeth. Honoring my parents means that I delight in them and acknowledge them with respect as people to whom I'm indebted more deeply than I could ever repay.

Disobeying Your Parents Third, some of the things our parents may desire or demand of us we must not do. So long as we live in their house, we're to abide by their rules. But we're not to abide by our parents' aspirations or expectations for us. We're to become ourselves. In this we are responsible not to our parents, but to God. If our parents' intentions for us conflict with what we believe to be God's will, the difference in our loyalties should be as great as love and hate. Some of Jesus' harshest words were that no person can be his disciple unless he's willing to hate his mother and his father (Lk 14:26).

While in high school, I planned to follow in my father's footsteps. I'd won a four-year scholarship to the University of Maryland to study electrical engineering and become a fire insurance executive. But I came to believe that God was calling me to enter the ministry instead. This completely contradicted my father's expectations for me. He couldn't understand why I was going to waste my life. He thought it was fanatical. But I had to refuse his expectations. It caused tremendous tension in my family which took about six years to heal. Recently my father has been struggling with multiple sclerosis and has begun to consider God more seriously. He now believes that God was trying to speak to him when I first became a Christian and took that stand. He feels that his rejection of God determined his harsh dealings with me at the time. And he's grateful that I refused to obey him and follow his expectations.

Having said all that, I find it interesting that this is the only one of the Ten Commandments that is stated positively. All the others are "thou shalt nots," but this one is a "thou shalt." It suggests to me that I'm being called on to go beyond the normal, everyday requirements of righteousness. Perhaps in the moment I feel I must disagree with my parents, I'm to honor them most deeply.

Think of the Future Fourth, this is the only one of the Ten Commandments with a promise attached to it. "Honor your father and your mother, that your days may be long. . . ." There isn't anything magical about that. It is a piece of straightforward, practical advice. A parable tells of a little old man who lived with his married son and daughter-in-law. His hands trembled, he had trouble eating, and he usually spilled things. So they made him a little table out in back. One day the couple noticed their own son playing with some bits of wood. They asked what he was doing, and he said, "I'm making a little table where I can feed you when I get big."

If you would like one day to be the sort of parent whose children find him honorable, you should begin today by being the sort of child who honors his parents.

John W. Howe, rector of Truro Episcopal Church in Fairfax, Virginia, is a former Inter-Varsity staff member. At the time he wrote this article he was chaplain of Miss Porter's School in Connecticut.

Family Feud

by R. Paul Stevens

3

There was a young man who cheated his brother, got everything he could out of his old man and then ran away to live with relatives. There he fell in love and got married, only to discover he had wed the wrong woman. He became a successful businessman, but something was eating away inside him. It had to do with his alienated brother, his strange name and his God.

It all started with the way he was born, coming forth from the womb grabbing the heel of his twin brother Esau. So they named him Jacob, which means "he who takes by the heel," as a wrestler pulls his opponent off balance by grabbing his heel. Cheater. Manipulator. Schemer. Imagine introducing yourself to a beautiful young woman when you've got a name like that. Jacob, true to his name, manipulated his brother out of the birthright by which the oldest son would inherit two-thirds of the estate (Gen 25:27-34); then he cheated him out of the blessing by which the promise to God's family would be passed on (27:1-40); he schemed to get the best of his father-in-law's flocks and herds by some dazzling genetic engineering (30:25-43); he tried to soften up his estranged brother with gifts (32:3-21). Jacob always had a plan, a scheme. Know anyone like that?

Jacob, Meet Jacob But God had a plan too. *And God's plan was first of all to bring Jacob to himself.* God wanted to bless Jacob, but he couldn't until Jacob came to terms with himself. Jacob was always running away from his own name (and his own nature) and therefore running away from God's blessing. Since Jacob would not admit his own name, God had to plot a series of scenes to hold up mirrors to his life:

Scene 1. God confronts Jacob with his own identity through his father's question: "Who are you, my son?" Jacob replies, "I am Esau your firstborn" (27:19). He plays a role (complete with costume contrived by his mother, Rebekah) to help him trick his father Isaac into blessing him. When Esau finds his blessing has been stolen, he wants to kill his brother. Exit Jacob.

Scene 2. Enter Rachel, a beautiful young woman by the well in the land to which Jacob has fled. Jacob will not tell Rachel his name. "And Jacob told Rachel that he was her father's kinsman and that he was Rebekah's son" (29:12). If my name was Cheat I wouldn't tell her either. But that is not the point. Jacob does not admit his character to anyone. Yet.

Scene 3. Enter Laban, his father-in-law. A polished mirror for Jacob. While Jacob thinks he is marrying Laban's youngest daughter, Rachel, Laban slips in walleyed Leah behind the veil. Just as Jacob dressed up in skins to imitate his brother, so Laban covers Leah to make Jacob think he has married Rachel. "What is this you have done to me?" (29:25). Jacob meets Jacob. A replay of the steal-the-blessing-from-your-brother act. Usually when we run away from home we end up pulling at the same old weeds in someone else's garden. If you're escaping into marriage, let that give you pause.

Scene 4. Jacob has to face the music. God calls him to return to his homeland (31:13)—return to brother Esau. Twenty years ago Esau wanted to kill him. Now Esau comes with four hundred men. Jacob prays! But he does some scheming too, as usual. Alone in the night, though, Jacob wrestles with God in the form of a man. Jacob is now a broken man. He has come to himself. The God-man asks him the question he has been avoiding for twenty years: "What is your name?" (32:27). And Jacob, for the first time in the entire account, speaks his own name.

"And he said, 'Jacob' " (32:27). Sounds too simple. Jacob must be *himself* before God. Not his brother. Not the Jacob he would like to be. No role playing. No vows and promises. No schemes and plans. No righteousness. Just "Jacob." He has to let God deal with the real Jacob, the self which God so patiently directed twenty years of conflicts to show him. Like the prodigal in Jesus' tale he can only come to the father if he comes to himself. Now he is no longer called Jacob but Israel. No longer "cheater," but "he strives with God." A new name and a new person. Limping and broken but knowing now that he belongs to God.

Reconciling the Rift *God's plan, secondly, was to bring Jacob to terms with his family.* If I were God and wanted to rescue the human race and reveal my own character, I would never think of doing it through a family. But if I did I'm sure I wouldn't choose this one, the family of Abraham, Isaac and Jacob (15:1-6). Not an ideal family, to say the least:

1. There was favoritism in it. "Isaac loved Esau, because he ate of his game; but Rebekah loved Jacob" (25:28). This resulted in envy, hostility and twenty years of separation between the brothers. Esau never felt accepted and tried pathetically to please his parents by his choice of wives (28:9)—some reason to get married! Jacob lapped up his mother's favoritism and learned to live that way, so he too had a favorite wife, Rachel (29:30), with the attendant envy, jealousy and alienation. Then he had a favorite child, Joseph, who was almost murdered by

his brothers. The sins of the fathers were visited upon the children unto the third and fourth generation.

2. The traditional family roles were reversed—Isaac was a weak leader; Rebekah, a strong and unsubmissive wife. Perhaps Isaac had married for the wrong reasons. He was over forty, and his mother had just died. (You can light a candle most easily just after it has been extinguished.) "Then Isaac brought her into the tent, and took Rebekah, and she became his wife; and he loved her. So Isaac was comforted after his mother's death" (24:67). The footnote tells us that he took her into his *mother's* tent. You can read between the lines. In spite of the prophecy that the elder son would serve the younger (25:23), Isaac went ahead and blessed his favorite. Rebekah lied and schemed against her husband to get him to bless her choice, Jacob (27:1-40).

3. There was alienation in that family—between parents, between sons, between wives, between children, between children and in-laws. Jacob left home with unresolved tensions with his parents and his brother. Twenty years of separation from family and therefore twenty years apart from God. No one can be right with God and wrong with his brother or sister.

4. But one more factor puts this family's story in the Bible. God was in that family. Where was he? Where wasn't he?

God had given his promise of blessing to this family and he would not revoke it (17:4ff.). For all the promises of God find their "Yes" in Christ (2 Cor 1:20).

God was simply with them, even though they did not know it. The runaway Jacob was given a vision of God's presence (28:10-22). The day after he cheated his brother, God said to him, "Behold, I am with you" (28:15). God graciously gave him the gift of faithful human love. "So Jacob served seven years for Rachel, and they seemed to him but a few days because of the love he had for her" (29:20). Most people won't wait even a few months to possess the object of their love. When Jacob prospered on his father-in-law's ranch, he had to admit it was God: "If the God of my father . . . had not been on my side . . . " (31:42). And then that dramatic night-encounter alone with the angel broke him and healed him. "For I have seen God face to face, and yet my life is preserved," he said (32:30). Even in the far country God never left him.

God Gives Homework God then took the members of this family through difficult lessons in reality to bring them to maturity and faith. Isaac was a worldly, sensuous man who loved to eat his hunter-son Esau's game. He lived to see Esau choose pagan wives that "made life bitter for Isaac and Rebekah" (26:35).

Rebekah, a scheming, manipulative wife with a favorite son, lost him from the family circle. Esau had contempt for his birthright and lost it and the blessing of the first-born son, though he later sought it with tears (Heb 12:17). Jacob, the heel-grabber, stole his brother's birthright and blessing. God let him have his way. But he had to run for his life, chased by his brother and always on the move. He was chased by his father-in-law (31:23). His only daughter was raped (34). His beloved and favorite wife died in childbirth (35:19). His favorite son, Joseph, was kidnapped and sold into slavery. God lets us have what we want.

But there is a surprise. Barren Rachel was miraculously given a child. Unloved and rejected Leah was chosen to continue the line of God's promise, and after Rachel died, Leah seems to have been loved.

Jacob? God graciously brought him to himself, a broken, limping but saved man. He was reconciled to his brother and saw in him the face of God (33:10).

God had brought them to the point of knowing that their needs could not be met by anyone but God himself. Each parent looked to a favorite child for satisfaction and was disappointed. Isaac looked to Esau, who made life bitter for him, and Rebekah looked to Jacob, who had to run for his life. Jacob got married but was still Jacob. Marriage did not solve his problems. It was when "Jacob was left alone" that he found God. No other idols. Remember the hard saying of Jesus to hate father, mother, wife and children to be his follower (Lk 14:26)? He must meet our needs. And he will introduce us to a bigger, better family (18:29-30).

God Calls Person-to-Person *Finally, God's plan was to bring Jacob to terms with God himself.* There is great inspiration in the phrase "the God of Abraham, Isaac and Jacob." In that is the seed of the gospel of Jesus who came not to call the righteous but sinners to repentance. God loves heel-grabbers and saves them. He is a God of grace. He works through the sensuality of Isaac, the scheming of Rebekah, the deception of Jacob. He is also a God who calls—and in his call is a promise. "Esau I have hated; Jacob I have loved" (Mal 1:2-3) hardly sounds like grace in the mouth of God. But God does not reject some in order to save others. In fact, he calls some in order to save everyone else who will hear the call. His call is not judgment but sheer mercy. We do not understand the inscrutable call of God but we see it illustrated in real life.

Esau seemed like the winner at the starting line—an all-around man. We'd place our bets on him. Like the elder brother in the parable of the prodigal son, he stayed home and did what his father wanted. But Esau was satisfied with his life as it was. He did not care for the promise of God. Jacob, on the other hand, cared so much for the promise that he would cheat to get it. He always wanted more. And he got it. But here is what Jacob had to undergo to come to terms with God.

First, he had to discover that he could not manipulate God. He had God well managed. He was too confident to be blessed. He could scheme his way through every situation to keep God well contained. He could make it through life on his own, he thought.

But he had to discover that he could not trust himself or his own work. At Bethel, God graciously met him as a runaway cheat. Jacob's response was a conditional vow: "If God will be with me . . . then the LORD shall be my God" (Gen 28:20). He had to face his brother in the end, but he contrived to win his favor with wave after wave of gifts (32:13).

Jacob had to want God and his blessing more than anything. Jacob came to the place of demanding the blessing of God. "I will not let you go, unless you bless me," he said to the angel. It was the first time he did not scheme. He was a beggar before God. No! A fighter of God, now fighting with God. People enter the kingdom by violence (Lk 16:16). Jesus said God is not for the mildly interested but for the desperate. Jacob would not let the night pass without God's blessing. And because of that he was given a new name, Israel, for he had "striven with God and with men *and have prevailed*" (32:28).

Finally Jacob had to clear his life of all that hindered worship of God. Twenty years after leaving home, the Hound of Heaven caught up with him. It was another ten years before Jacob kept his vow to return to Bethel and build an altar. He put away foreign gods and purified himself and family to live a life of worship.

Jacob finished well. We would have chosen Esau. But God chose Jacob and Jacob finished with God, the God of Abraham, Isaac and Jacob, the God and Father of our Lord Jesus Christ. The God who loves heel-grabbers.

Paul Stevens, former Inter-Varsity staff member in Canada, works part-time in construction. He is a teaching elder at Marineview Chapel in Vancouver.

Dear Dad

by Jeanne Doering Zornes

4

I couldn't hide the tears that poured down my cheeks as I wrote.

"What's wrong?" my college roommate asked as she walked over to my desk.

"I just wrote a very important letter to my dad," I answered, blotting my face. "Things out of the depths of the heart come hard."

It was September 24. Five days later, on the twenty-ninth, my dad would sit alone on what would have been his thirty-eighth wedding anniversary.

This anniversary, Mom was gone. Her battle with cancer had ended in early summer. I knew Dad's aloneness would be difficult. I had spent the last part of the summer with him, but I felt I had to go ahead with plans to start graduate school that fall, 2,400 miles away. Leaving was difficult. He had hugged me tightly and wept as he prayed for a safe journey for me.

There had been times in recent years when I resisted hugging him. I'd been hurt deeply by a fractured romance, so for a while it was hard for me to relate to any man. But as God brought emotional healing, he showed me the strong character of my dad.

Soul Provider Before I was born, Dad had surrendered a secure job as a chemist in Washington State to move to southern California where doctors said Mom's chronic asthma would improve. Although a college graduate, he sold kitchen pans and vacuum cleaners door-to-door until he was able to get work in his profession.

He insisted on being the family's sole provider. He never wanted Mother to have to work if she didn't want to, and she never did. He encouraged her in her sewing and art hobbies, even helping her tie quilts and mark hems. He had a giving spirit and was often the one who helped the widows in our town by visiting them and doing minor home repair.

I saw more of his tender heart as cancer drained away Mom's life. I remember watching him at her deathbed, reading to her from Psalm 116 ("Precious in the sight of the LORD is the death of his saints") and then faithfully holding her swollen hand until his head dropped in exhausted sleep.

Now he faced probably the loneliest day of his grief. I wanted to tell him I loved him and that I was thankful for him. I'd been reading through Paul's letters in the New Testament. Over and over, the apostle had expressed thanks:

"I do not cease to give thanks for you" (Eph 1:16). "I thank my God in all my remembrance of you" (Phil 1:3). "We always thank God, the Father of our Lord Jesus Christ, when we pray for you" (Col 1:3). "I thank God whom I serve with a clear conscience, as did my forefathers when I remember you constantly in my prayers" (2 Tim 1:3).

Affirmative Action If Paul could tell his spiritual children how thankful he was for them, why couldn't I tell my dad how thankful I was for him? Many times, of course, I'd told Dad that I loved him. But now, more than ever, he needed that affirmation. He needed to know why. And so I wrote that letter. It carried a message I could not have delivered in person. I learned later that he cried when he got the letter. And he shared it with a few close friends. Ten weeks later he died of a heart attack.

Dropping out of school to take care of affairs, I faced the huge task of cleaning out the family home. As I dumped out drawers and sorted through the piles of mail, I remembered the anniversary letter. Had he kept it? Dad usually saved everything of sentimental value. Or had the letter upset him so much that he destroyed it?

January passed, then February as I slowly sorted out his and mother's personal belongings. I found old birthday cards, my grade-school papers and letters ten and fifteen years old. But not *that* letter. Then in March I got to the closet where luggage was stored. There it was, in the pocket of the suitcase he used on a trip the week before his death.

He had kept it with him.

Love Letter I opened it and cried again, thankful I'd written when I did:

"Dear Daddy, I know this will be a very lonely September 29 for you without Mom. I wish I could be there to comfort you. I greatly miss her, too, and as I write this the tears are coming so fast I have to blot my face every few words. I don't know what it's like to celebrate an anniversary with the one you love. Though I would desire to be married, God has not granted that privilege yet. But he did grant it to you and Mom, and along with it he sent the sorrows and joys that stretched you, refined you and perfected you.

"I wasn't there, only a plan in God's mind, when Mom's health necessitated the move to California in the early 1940s. But I look back on that move as one illustration of a man who—despite the fragile uncertainties of the future—honored his commitment to love and care for his wife. That takes a special man.

"The Lord, knowing Mom's needs, was infinitely wise when he brought you two together and assigned Mom's care to you (and your care, likewise, to her). And that is merely the beginning of the story, because when he gave you two daughters, he deemed you worthy of caring for them too.

"I can't help believing that the Lord has more tasks for you as you have now greater resources in abilities and time than ever before. And he will show you what those tasks are to be.

"But while we wait—either for the hope of his calling or (maranatha!) the hope of his *coming*—we can wait confidently that neither death nor life . . . things present nor things to come . . . in fact, *nothing* 'will be able to separate us from the love of God, in Christ Jesus our Lord' (Rom 8:39).

"I love you in a deep way. . . and God loves you infinitely. Jeanne."

Each sentence had been hard to put down. I had hidden my gratitude too long.

But I'm thankful that God prompted me to send that note of love—in time.

Jeanne Doering Zornes is a former assistant editor of Moody Monthly, *the publication in which this article originally appeared.*

My Sister

Name Withheld

5

Friends with my sister? Impossible.

You'll probably say I'm just making excuses, but we really don't have that much in common. I know, I know, we were born of the same parents, grew up in the same house, went to the same church, and attended the same school. But we're opposites.

As a child Ann always read books while I played outside with the kids and got grounded for coming home late. When I asked her to play baseball or go for a walk, she'd always refuse. Finally I gave up and stopped asking her.

I will admit, though, that in the last few years I have begun to realize there actually are some similarities between us. But the characteristics we have in common seem to be the ones that cause our greatest conflicts! We're both stubborn, full of pride, and easily offended. During our college years when we'd be home together after months of separation at rival universities, we'd get along great—for the first hour.

Room and Bored There was one thing about me that really used to upset my sister. She noticed how I would sit and listen to my friends for hours, giving them my undivided attention. As soon as they left I'd start my studying. Ann would come into the room, excited to share some of the latest facts she'd learned in her pet hobby, British history. As she looked up from the article she was sharing, to make sure I was really listening, she'd discover that I'd left the room, books and all, to seek a quieter place to study. I'm afraid this happened more than once.

Finally Ann confronted me with tears in her eyes. "How come you can sit there and listen to your friends for an hour, and when I want to talk to you for a few minutes, you say you don't have time or you're not interested, and leave the room?"

The answer was easy: "What interests my friends interests me, because I care about them."

There was an awkward pause in the conversation. I quickly realized how Ann was interpreting that last comment—I knew by the crestfallen look on her face. I said, "Oh, Ann, you know I love you. You're my sister."

She wasn't convinced and I'm not sure I was either. I didn't realize it then, but I was about to begin a long pilgrimage.

Faraway Places I was a Christian. God had redeemed me and given me a new life. I wanted to devote my life to him. After college I went to South America for a year of short-term missionary work. Lots happened during that year away, even in my relationship with Ann.

I'd write her about all that God was doing in people's lives and how God could grow in her life. Her answer was, "Why should I believe anything you say?" At first I was offended by her response to my good intentions, but then I began to ask myself, "Why should she believe me?" I thought of all the ways I hadn't expressed Christian love to her. It occurred to me that until I apologized for my past behavior and began to show her true love, she would continue to consider me the hypocrite I had been.

After thinking about it for a long time, I humbled myself before God and my sister and wrote a letter. I apologized for the many things I had done to hurt her and pledged to change my behavior. After I mailed it, I got excited. It felt good, having set things straight.

Mail from North America was slow, but finally, there was Ann's handwriting. Her response was, "I'll believe it when I see it." Anger and hurt welled up within me; then I cooled off and admitted that this was exactly the chance I had asked for.

My year abroad passed quickly and I was determined to go back and love my sister. When I got there, I made lots of noble efforts; but they never seemed to turn out the way I intended.

Broken Connection For example, one evening I decided to splurge and call her long distance, just to chat and let her know I was thinking about her. I checked the time, 11:30. When we were home together on weekends she always watched the Johnny Carson prologue so I figured she'd still be up.

I dialed. The phone rang twice. Then there was a faint hello. I greeted her cheerily and asked how she was. An icy silence followed. Then she said, and her voice was no longer faint, "You knew I'd be in bed, why did you call?" She then proceeded to tell me how thoughtless I had been toward my parents about something, and what a thoughtless person I was all the time.

She stopped for a second to see what I would say. When there was no response she realized she had gone a little too far. I was crushed. The love I had mustered up to make the call had dissolved and I was left empty inside. She asked anxiously why I wasn't saying anything. I told her that I was sorry, but I didn't have anything left to say. We exchanged stiff good-byes.

At that point I was desperate. I fell to my knees and said to God, "If you want me to love her, you're going to have to provide the love because I just don't have enough. I've tried my best and I give up."

New Resource God had waited a long time for me to discover that I couldn't do this all by myself. God loves to transform relationships, and I knew at that moment he was capable of transforming even this one that I had worked on so hard and botched up so badly. He would be my guide on this pilgrimage of friendship. I realized how foolish and helpless I had been, trying to do it alone.

Many months have passed since the Lord began to intervene. I still have to remind myself to let the Lord do the loving; the journey is hard, but I've seen changes.

I'm learning to listen to Ann as a friend because I love her. I'm exposing myself to her interests and actually learning from her areas of expertise. As I was going out for a walk one pretty morning, she astonished me by saying she'd come with me. We had a really good talk.

She's going for walks with me often now, and I'm not so reluctant to share with her some of the rough spots in my life. We're learning to confide in each other.

The pilgrimage isn't over, but at least I'm not walking alone now. The Lord and my sister are accompanying me on the journey.

Part 2
Evangelism Family Style

Home: How to Be Salt to Your Family without Rubbing It In

by Janet Carter

6

If you ever want to know what it is like to have a sledgehammer held over your head in the name of Jesus, just talk to any member of my family! But if you want to know some of God's mercy, grace and faithfulness in my witness to my once-born family, read on.

Some of our fears of witness and/or compromise as we face the prospect of going home to an unbelieving family for an extended visit are unfortunately misplaced. And our energies are often misdirected at home as we either argue with or seek to win points by frantic service to our fellow heirs and parent(s). Whether it be fear or fanaticism, neither will be a very effective medium for transmitting the love and grace of the Lord.

Concerning our family life, we should regard ourselves not as missionaries going to pagan foreign soil, but as ambassadors entering a host country, where courtesy, respect, sensitivity and magnanimity are in order. This is the imagery of Scripture and the reality of our mission. We may face ticklish situations; in fact, we do wage much more than a "cold war" with human ideas in that our battle is with a host of spiritual forces. However, the One who appoints and sends us is the rightful King and he already reigns in heaven.

Losing Face and Faith "Perfect love casts out fear." If we fear—whether the object be personal compromise, "falling away," persecution, or having to explain our position as a Christian—we will not love. Now the question is, do you want to love your family? Do you experience the love of Christ yourself? Do you desire for them to see him in and through you? God's love can cast away our fears and keep us from falling.

Once upon a time (and in space, of course) God, in his great mercy, swallowed all his glory and postponed his rights as King in order to give us his only Son. For a time he willingly gave him to us, sending him to this cold, spiritually barren earth to be an example of perfect love in the face of ridicule and scorn, to endure loneliness and pain, and ultimately to die in the shame of unwarranted criminal execution. All this that we might be healed and restored to God's fellowship with Jesus in his resurrection power.

Does this sound like a cheap God? Like someone who can't relate to your fears or your unique family situation? He knows it all and has ample resources to prepare you and sustain you in your time at home. He even wants to spread his love through you to those around you, as a "fragrance of beauty."

Weird Wonder "But," you say, "my parents will never understand my position and my brothers and sisters will think I'm positively weird." Well, do *you* think it's weird that you are a Christian? Or are you convinced that you have landed onto Someone pretty wonderful?

I finally said to myself, "Face it. If your parents have cried in concern over you, paid your medical bills, fed and clothed you for all these years, they aren't going to pounce on you *now,* now that you claim to have discovered something that promises to satisfy you completely." I once asked my mother what hopes she had for me, deep down inside, thinking that she probably hoped for me to follow in her profession, or to go to grad school and become a lawyer or something equally amazing. However, she replied thoughtfully that what she wanted most for me was my complete happiness ("though of course I wouldn't mind having grandchildren some day," she added sneakily—mothers are like that).

The catch is, of course, that to really convince your loved ones you're happy, you have to *be* happy. My brother used to complain that all I ever did when I was home from school was read and study. A few months ago as I grabbed brother #1 and teased him into teaching me the latest dance, both brothers were sure I had gone nuts. But they saw a freer, more joyful sister than they ever had during my years of concentrated spirituality.

Most parents do want to see their children be deeply satisfied. That does not mean lazy or self-righteous, uncaring or disrespectful. You will most helpfully mirror the love of Jesus to your parents, brothers and sisters as you are grateful to God for the unique family he has given you, daily grateful for a free gift of salvation in the Lord Jesus Christ, and delighted at every opportunity you can grasp to learn more of life, of people and of our God.

Remember: Assume they love you unless proven otherwise. Parents, just like you and me, have trouble expressing deep feelings. They, too, feel inadequate at times to be totally consistent in their actions.

We are called to honor and obey our parents. Webster defines honor to include "giving credit to" and "giving reverence where it is due." Let's say your dad's eyes roam a bit to other women and your mom curses and shouts. Does God expect you to respect these qualities and actions? Certainly not. We are not to rejoice in iniquity, but in the truth and in godliness. But it is the Lord's responsibility to deal with the particular sins and shortcomings of your parents, just as with your own. He is the one who knows their hearts, their histories, and their circumstances. We are to celebrate *his* life, not legislate theirs. And almost always there are some things in each parent which we can respect.

A critical attitude is powerful to destroy the relationship God has in mind for you and your parents. And no attitudes are picked up more quickly by parent radar than ingratitude and bitterness. They eat away at love and trust, and they hurt parents deeply. We forget all they have done for us, while presuming they will continue to do it. We self-righteously and with complaints compare ourselves to our brothers and sisters. We forget that Mom and Dad are regular human beings, with personal hopes, tender spots and insecurities. They are not perfect parents and we're not perfect offspring. We must not hold it against them.

That Strange Habit Or is your fear one of losing touch with God and his Word? This can be disarmed to some extent as you understand the basic issue. You must determine *now,* before you go home for a visit, how important your quiet times alone with the Lord are. You may face occasional or repeated pressure to neglect your Bible, or to avoid worship. If your family is offended by a Bible, will you hide it and forget about it, or will you quietly take it to the library to read? How determined are you and how creative will you be? How much in love are you with Christ?

Sometimes we hit periods when our relationship with Jesus is really not all that exciting or productive. Students, is summertime a secretly welcomed occasion for you to take a vacation from him too? Be honest. If it is, tell him now and ask him to change you. He loves you no matter whether or how much you love him.

Actually, when it comes to family response, your approach to quiet time and Bible reading is much more essential than the actual activity. If your attitude is "devotional" or "spiritual," it will be more resented than if you are simply matter-of-fact about the whole thing. My stepsister came to me one evening while I was visiting at home and asked what I was reading. I answered lightly, "the Good Book!" and folded it in my lap temporarily to chat with her. At first she was a bit surprised, and then, because I took it so naturally, she took it naturally. Of course, there were the days not so awfully long ago when I would hole myself up in "my" room to have quiet time, and even though I put up no signs, PRIVACY PLEASE just oozed out from behind the tightly closed door. My mother would sort of tiptoe around the hall trying to find a place to put my clean, folded clothes but also trying to figure out what in the world made her nunnish daughter tick. Here I was, supposedly loving God and serving people, yet my mom was serving me and I was making it difficult. Your privacy is not sacred, nor do you have a right to expect it in your parents' home. Remember that Jesus had to get up long before daybreak and go out to a lonely place to pray. Ask him for some good ideas—he's been there.

Remember, too, that you are reading a collection of historical writings and Hebrew literature, not to mention four pieces of a unique literary genre: the Gospels. Your parents and family might possibly relate more to this explanation than to the comment that you are reading a Holy Book that is God-breathed, infallible and utterly reliable. You can explain that there is some really great literature in this anthology, and that in presenting what God is like it gives you some very useful teaching on being the person you're intended to be—achieving your potential. Pray that God will guard you from compromise, but remember that (like Jesus and Paul) we speak in different "languages" to different mindsets and understandings.

Head Bowed, Eyes Closed Another cloudy area surrounds the questions of conversation and activity in the home. Should you say grace before your meal, even if your family is convinced it just came from the supermarket? What about wine at meals? Theological arguments? Going shopping with your insistent mother to buy piles of new clothes? And on Sunday, no less? Whew! For one thing, the Lord doesn't expect you to answer them all at once. And again, the attitude with which you join in or decline the activities at hand will make a huge difference in the response of your family.

If you already have a reputation in your family for being pushy or legalistic, I'd heartily suggest going easy on the outward expressions of your spirituality. You may have to spend some time convincing your loved ones (by your naturalness) that you really are free in Christ, and that Christianity is not just another varied collection of "do's and don'ts." When I was a fairly new Christian, I would insist that we pray before eating (while my two younger brothers squirmed) and then when my uncomfortable mother would resort to always asking *me* to "do it," I would be offended: "Can't anyone else pray?" Well, do I need to tell you that what my family remembers about those days is not my overflowing, grateful attitude which bubbled over in a desire to pray at every opportunity, but my unhappy, restricted self. Again, though, God's mercy is abundant, and now, several years later, I can see my mistake and also his healing. Last Christmas, after I had taken the opportunity to get to know my new stepfather-to-be and shared my Christian perspective on life with him, as well as some doubts and struggles I was having, I was incredulous when he asked me if I wouldn't like to say grace at our first Christmas meal together. (I was thankful for a lot more than the gorgeous meal we had at our table that day.)

Who Can You Trust? What about going to non-Christian friends or relatives with personal questions and hassles? What do you share and what do you bear? Perhaps you do not anticipate having much Christian fellowship and support while at home, and think you'll have to have at least a three-hour quiet time daily to work through your problems. Well, for one thing, you probably won't have a three-hour quiet time. Second, unless you are transparent about your problems or doubts, they will be revealed in less straightforward ways—you can't really fool your family. Third, all truth is God's truth, and much wise counsel can be given by people who are "still on the way" spiritually but whose general maturity and experience of life make them wise. Trust God to help you use their counsel correctly.

During the time shortly after I graduated from high school and before I finally went on to college, I had many personal questions regarding my fatherlessness (my mother was widowed when I was a small child). I was experiencing emotional upheaval upon having to face my future without any inkling whatsoever of what I wanted to do with my life. And I wondered if I really wanted to hassle the whole thing anyway.

Part of my reluctance to share all this was because I felt my mother was having enough problems of her own raising us three kidlings alone, and perhaps this was justified. But it never occurred to me that some sort of discussion with Mom or one of my brothers might aid me in my struggles. I was sure I had to do it all alone, with the help of the Lord, of course, and was afraid that any admission of problems would ruin the chances of their coming to Christ.

Besides the fact that no one comes to repentance by chance, this attitude is really a false spirituality. My aloofness cheated my family of two important things during this period: a knowledge of me, their "only girl," *and* a clear understanding in their minds that it was not my acclaimed Lord who was having all these hassles; rather, it was me.

It Shows I'll never forget the day I walked away from my mother after we'd had some tense moments talking about all the many Christian activities I was attending. (At the time I was involved in a weekly breakfast Bible study, church three times a week, and a coffeehouse ministry on the weekends. For someone who had once been enmeshed in everything from kite-flying conventions to social work, this was not normal at all.) Mom told me that from what she saw around the house, she knew I couldn't possibly be happy. I wasn't, of course, but how dreadful that she could see it. I was offended because it was ridiculous (so I thought) to suppose that a Christian should be unhappy. I was frustrated because my family didn't seem to perceive that I had eternal, abundant life—that I had nothing to worry about anymore.

You might as well be open about your frustrations and fears around those dear ones who share your towels and toothpaste, because you will never successfully hide them. Pray for greater faith to entrust them to the Lord so you don't have to burden your family (or your Christian family) with your problems; but until you grow in faith and grace, you'd better be honest. You may bring some of their deep-seated questions to the surface also and perhaps open the way for them to find answers in the Lord. Being strong doesn't mean being perfect—it means knowing some of the answers and a lot of the questions, and living on what you have. As we are strong in our security with the Lord, we can relax with our families.

You will miss some of the most fruitful times of friendship and growth with your family if you go home fearing "contamination" or "falling away." What God requires is that we walk humbly with him and seek to do justice. He does not appreciate religious overtures and "spiritual" favors. He does not appreciate our worry. What he desires is our complete attention, our willingness to keep in close touch with him, to discuss doubtful situations, and to be repentant when he convicts us in our spirits.

If you have a tendency to make your Christian life complicated, your parents, brothers and sisters will be the first to be misled by the smokescreen you put up. If you are honest, they will eventually see the difference God is making in the way you handle life. Relax.

Janet Carter has been a program coordinator at Hollygrove, a children's home in Los Angeles. She is a graduate of the University of California at Santa Barbara.

Facing Your Parents for the First Time . . . since Your Second Birth

by Ward Patterson

7

It was one of those touching moments in life. They helped carry the stereo up the long flights of steps into the little dorm room that would be Phyllis's home for the nine months.

The stereo was followed by blue and avocado suitcases and loads of multicolored clothes drooping limply over arms to catch black hangers on banisters and doorknobs. Soon all was deposited in the little cubicle, the roommate was met and inspected, and the time came for her parents to leave Phyllis to the mercy of the university.

What Will Happen to Our Freshman? As they headed home in the family station wagon, Phyllis's parents thought silently of what lay ahead for their daughter. Would she be able to cope with the drug and drink pressures? Would she be able to handle the sex scene? Would she be able to cut it in her classes?

How would she change during the next four years? Would she enjoy her college years? Would they be proud of her? Had they advised her correctly in her choice of school and major?

But that was last fall. Now it is Christmas and Phyllis is home from college. Left behind are the small cubicle in the dorm and the "university bland" dorm meals. Phyllis clomps over the threshold, tracking snow as she used to do when she was a small girl. Her father and her mother remember and they are glad to see the snow again on the rug.

Talk flows quickly, of college, of guys, of brothers and sisters. And then Phyllis, eyes shining, tells her parents, "The most wonderful thing has happened!"

The Bombshell "She's engaged and I didn't even suspect it," her mother thinks.

"She's finally made up her mind what her major is going to be," her father reasons.

"I've accepted Christ as my Savior," Phyllis says, "And I've become a Christian."

"But you were always a Christian," her mother says. "We christened you when you were about a month old."

"I know, but now I have accepted Christ myself and I really want him to be first in my life."

"The Moonies have gotten hold of her," her mother thinks, panicking.

"She's become a Jesus freak," her father shudders.

Phyllis bubbles on about the Christian love and fellowship she has found on campus, noting only gradually the gray gloom that has begun to settle on her father's face. "Religion is fine," he says, trying to be conciliatory, "as long as you don't go overboard on it."

"I hope these Jesus friends of yours aren't interfering with your having a good time at college," her mother interjects, nervously stirring the gravy. "College is one of the freest times of your life and you should try all kinds of things."

Phyllis begins to sense that her faith is somehow threatening to her parents. They are nominal members of a large church in town. They attend now and then, but Christ has never been spoken about much in the home, except at Christmas. Phyllis senses that the most important news in her life is being heard with condescension by her parents.

"I was once really active in our youth group," her mother says. "But then I sort of grew out of it. You're probably just passing through a stage."

Case #2 Phil's arrival at the university was no big deal. Phil had had his own car since he was sixteen. His mom and dad had never been to college and they couldn't care less whether he went or not. He had not been on speaking terms with his stepmother for the past six months, ever since he moved out of the house and went on his own. He respected his father, but had never really been able to talk with him. Phil was going to prove himself to his parents—prove his worth and his value. He was going to show them that he could amount to something.

But that was last fall. Now, just before Christmas, Phil returns from college. He has become a Christian, and one of the things he has learned from the teaching of his college fellowship group is that he should let Christ root out the bitterness in his life.

And there is a lot of that to be rooted out in Phil. He resents his stepmother and he recalls the bitterness of past encounters with her. He comes home fearfully this Christmas, afraid that his Christianity will not stand up to the test. Will he end up once again where he has always been before, shouting and hurting?

"I love you, Sarah," he says to his stepmother shortly after returning home. The words sound strange and insincere. "I'm sorry for the way I've treated you in the past." Phil isn't sure whether he is sorry or not, actually, but he goes on, "I want there to be love in this home, Christ's love. I've taken Christ as my

Savior and I want to love because of his love for me."

Sarah looks at him in disbelief, then responds, "What are you up to now?"

Phil's father comes into the kitchen, on his way to the refrigerator for a beer. He catches the end of the conversation before heading back toward the TV set and the football game. "Get this," Sarah says to him in derision, "if Phil ain't gone to college and got religion!"

"Yeh?" says Phil's father. "We got any more cold beer?"

Watch Out for the Fanatics Variations on these two stories occur in countless lives. Each year thousands of young people head for college. Thousands of parents worry about what the college years are going to do to their children. And many parents are shocked with the news that something, in their eyes worse than drunkenness, immorality, drugs or failure, has come into the lives of their children. That something is committed Christian faith.

No two relationships between parents and children are the same. So it is hard to generalize as to how a Christian can best relate to his or her non-Christian home. Some parents are nominal Christians for whom church is merely a social organization. They will have a hard time handling a child who takes the Bible and its teaching as a serious guide for daily life. Religion is fine, but let's not get carried away.

Other parents are openly hostile toward Christianity. Their lifestyle has no place in it for the absolutes of God. Religion to them is at best a crutch and at worst an unwanted impingement on personal freedom.

Guidelines Even though situations vary, let us consider some guidelines for sharing one's faith with non-Christian parents.

1. *Pray for them.* Pray for them regularly and earnestly. Pray not only that they will accept you and your faith, but that God will use you to speak to their deepest needs. Examine their lives

and discern what those deepest hungers and thirsts are. Pray for their blind spots. Thank God for their strengths. James 5:16 (KJV) tells us, "The effectual fervent prayer of a righteous man availeth much." And Jesus said, "If you abide in me, and my words abide in you, ask whatever you will, and it shall be done for you" (Jn 15:7). Pray for them on the way to class. Pray for them with other Christians.

On our campus, about a dozen students began getting together to pray for their non-Christian parents. It strengthened each of them to learn that they were not alone in their situation. It helped them to learn how others were attempting to share Christ at home. Their prayers were earnest and direct, and the students began to see evidence of God's answers in their relationships with their parents.

On at least one occasion, when a student phoned her parents during a particularly difficult confrontation, other students were praying in the next room for her and her conversation. She hugged her praying friends when she hung up. It was the first conversation she had had in months that had not ended in angry tears.

Pray for wisdom and discernment. Ask God to help you see yourself as your parents see you so you can understand their reactions to you and your faith. Pray that you will be able to share your faith without conveying a "holier than thou" attitude to your parents. Pray that you will have true Christian humility and that you will be able to communicate to them your love.

2. As you pray, *examine your own past actions and attitudes* in light of the teaching of Jesus. Are there things you need to make amends for?

Have you responded to tensions by developing a pattern of being hurtful and hateful toward your parents? Do you share certain sour memories of occasions when you lashed out, stomped out, sulked, or otherwise punished your parents? Is there something you can do now to undo some of the past? Take the initiative to break down the barriers of the past by seeking forgiveness for *your* part, even if you aren't the only one at fault.

3. *Work at more open communication* with your parents in all areas of your life, not just in the area of your faith. Begin to share with them on as many levels as possible. Confide in them your fears and your triumphs. Write often. Letters are valued by parents more than students can know. Write often, even if briefly. Share the small details of your life as well as the important things. Let them in on who you are.

Listen carefully to what your parents say, noting the values from which they speak. Listen not only to what they are saying, but also to what is behind what they are saying. They may say something like, "We want you to be careful that you don't get tied up with some strange religious group." What lies behind this may be a sincere concern for your good. Recognizing this concern will enable you to reassure your parents that you have not been brainwashed on campus.

4. *Let them see what Christ means* in your life. Try to be the best son or daughter you can be. They will respect your Jesus only if they see that he is making you a better person.

As Christians, we must build a bridge of trust and appreciation to our parents if it does not already exist. We would expect to do this in sharing our faith with a stranger—it is all the more important with our parents who know our weaknesses so well. We must show by our lives that we have something worthy of being listened to.

How can you do this? Remember them. Remember their birthdays and anniversaries. Give them gifts of thoughtfulness. Remember their likes and dislikes and surprise them now and then. Let them know that they remain important in your life even if you are separated.

Do we take it for granted that our parents owe us a college education? Do we ever express appreciation for the sacrifices they make for us? Do we do our best to use the money we receive wisely? Do we show maturity in all our dealings? Do we look for ways to relieve them from the burden of looking after our material needs or do we exploit their generosity? Do we show in significant ways that we respect their rights as parents?

One idea: On your next birthday, send your folks a thank-you card for all they have given to you during these X years of your life.

5. *Be patient with them.* Realize that they may test the reality of your faith. They may test its strength against their criticism and belittlement. They may try to see how soon they can get you to return to your old patterns. They will want to see just what your faith is made of. (Why shouldn't they?) If, in love, your faith withstands and flourishes, it will be the more powerful witness to them.

Many of us want to win our parents in the first conversation about Jesus. That may occasionally happen, but it is more likely that our parents will put our faith to the test over a period of time before they are ready to take serious note of its true value.

Remember that when light comes into darkness, those who are used to darkness are uncomfortable. Your faith may seem threatening to your parents for it exposes their deeds and attitudes. It is extremely important that you come to them in humility and love. Still, some parents will choose to interpret your faith as rejection of them. That is why you must take pains to convey love in as many ways as possible without compromising your faith.

Replaced! For seventeen years or more, your parents have been the voice of wisdom and experience in your life. They have been your prime reference point for knowledge and truth. Now you say that Christ has become that reference point. What a put-down! To parents who don't understand what his lordship means, it can be very threatening. Assure them their importance in your life has not diminished.

Another shift: You are developing to the point where you can be their peer in many areas. It is difficult for them to accept that you might well be able to teach them something of lasting importance, you who have always come to them for answers.

It may be helpful for you to share with them the process by which you came to faith, as well as the result of the process. They may well be unaware of the problems you have been facing and the insights that have gone into your decision. Thus, what you know has been thoughtfully and seriously undertaken may seem to them to be sudden and capricious. The joy, peace and assurance you have in Christ will be more comprehensible to your parents if they can follow with you the step-by-step process by which you came to Christ.

Chapters 2 and 3 of 1 Peter give a lot of advice on living as a Christian in relationships. Consider making a study of this passage with yourself and your parents in mind. List specific things you can do which will both please the Lord and help your folks get an accurate picture of what the Lord is like.

Then work at being the most honest and loving son or daughter you can be to them—and leave the rest to him.

Ward Patterson has worked with Christian students at Indiana University, Bloomington.

Parable of the Lost Parents

by Sharon Sheppard

8

And it came to pass that a certain young man went away to a far country to college, and there he met the Master. After a time he began to be greatly distressed over the unregenerate condition of his parents.

Now his parents were goodly parents, loving and kind. And they were moved with compassion toward their son, even when he was afar off. Yea, they were even paying part of the young man's tuition. His mother wrote him weekly epistles, and often sent him special victuals she prepared in her own kitchen.

The young man began earnestly to beseech the Master to convict his parents of their sins, and daily he prayed for their salvation with great fervor. But at last he grew impatient, for it seemed to him that his prayers were in vain, and so he began to devise all manner of plans for bringing them into the kingdom.

Now the time for great feasting drew near, and the young man said to himself, "I will arise and go to my parents and set them straight." And so he clothed himself in his Jesus T-shirt, tucked his Living Bible under his arm, and set out on the long journey to his parents' farm.

Now when he arrived, his parents rejoiced at seeing their son, and they threw their arms around him and kissed him and welcomed him home.

Wasting no time the young man said, "Father and Mother, you have sinned against God and against heaven, and you are not worthy to be called his children. But if you will repent of your wicked ways, the Master will forgive you and will welcome you into his fold."

Now the parents were sore dismayed, for they belonged to the synagogue and attended it regularly. It was true that they had never made a personal commitment of their lives to the Master, but they were good people, and had observed the rituals of the temple from their youth up. And so they were sore offended. Now the climate of the household grew cold and hostile, and so the young man cut his visit short and returned to the campus deeply sorrowful.

As the time for the young man's birthday drew near, he again made his way home to visit his family. His parents had gathered a bountiful supply of gifts, and his mother had prepared a wonderful feast in his honor. Truly this is the opportunity the Master has prepared for me to be a witness to my family, the young man thought. So he attached a "The Rapture: The Only Way to Fly" bumper sticker to his chariot, and pinned his large "Heaven or Hell? Turn or Burn" button to his cloak, and when all of his relatives had gathered, he boldly took his stand for the Master, and made plain the way of salvation.

After the feast he gave tracts to all who had gathered, and went back to the campus rejoicing in the opportunity the Lord had provided, earnestly praying for the Lord to convict his relatives of their sins.

Now the young man wrote home to his parents often that

winter (though it was usually to ask for money), and though he felt he had been persecuted for righteousness' sake by their cool reception to his testimony, he remained faithful in reminding his parents of their need for repentance in each of his letters.

There were times during the year when his parents became unreasonably demanding of his presence, and the young man grew righteously indignant. One morning his father called to him when his mother was in the hospital to suggest that it would gladden her heart if he could come home for the weekend. But the season for exams was approaching and the young man was sorely behind in his studies, having been exceedingly zealous in the Lord's work. And so he could not come.

And again his mother called to him and pleaded with him to come to his grandparents' golden wedding feast, but alas, it conflicted with the church banquet, where he longed to have fellowship with his brothers and sisters in Christ. And so he bought a beautiful anniversary card with a spiritual message, tucked in a $2 bill (which he could ill afford, having spent almost all of his goods on a new set of Scripture memorization tapes), and wrote his grandparents a note saying how sorry he was to miss their feast, and that he would be praying that they would yield to the Master now in the golden years of their lives before it was too late.

Now it came to pass in the spring of the year, when his father needed help in planting his crops, that he wrote to his son and asked him to come home and help. But the young man replied, "Father, you know how I would like to be able to do what you ask, but I must do the will of my Heavenly Father. This is the weekend of our fellowship's retreat, and I must tend to the needs of my soul. Perhaps my older brother will help you." And so the older brother, who had not met the Master, willingly went and did his father's bidding.

And so the years of the young man's university career passed quickly by, and though he saw less and less of his family, he never failed to remember them in his prayers.

And the young man grew strong in his beliefs and memorized much Scripture and enjoyed a wealth of fellowship with like-minded believers.

Sharon Sheppard teaches English at Area Vocational Technical Institute in St. Cloud, Minnesota.

Jeremiah the Bullfrog and Other Tools for Sibling Evangelism

Name Withheld

9

I have a brother. He's probably the person I love most in the world, and he's one of my best friends. We get along quite well, which surprises people (it shouldn't) because he's not a Christian.

What I long for most, and pray for more consistently than anything else, is that he would come to know Christ. Longing and praying for him for several years have provided much time to think through the best ways to communicate the gospel of Christ to non-Christian siblings. Witnessing hinges on loyal friendships which are becoming rare in families in North America. Here are some ideas about transcending the barriers that often exist between Christians and non-Christians in a family.

Friendship with non-Christian siblings begins as we establish credibility as a person. My brother once paid my roommate and me a compliment I'll never forget: "You two are the only Christians I respect because you talk like normal people." (I've made sure since then that he's met others.)

I've continued to try to be fully human around him. I show emotions, whether right or wrong, and share problems, joys and hassles with him. It's important that he knows I'm a struggling person, and that my chief allegiance is not to a code of moral ethics. Instead, I belong to a Lord who illuminates daily battles. It's not necessary to share deep theological problems that are plaguing me, yet I do tell him about my frequent roommate hassles. I also talk a lot with him about my desires and fears concerning marriage. Non-Christians need to see that we have struggles just as they do. Being a Christian doesn't, or shouldn't, mean living in a sterile box, isolated from real life.

With our brothers and sisters we have a unique chance to be vulnerable, human, real people. They've known us for years, and we spend lots of time day in and day out with them, even if it's just during vacations. Opening up to them is often threatening. It might mean coming down off the pedestal we've been living on. Yet it is vitally important to our credibility as people that we show some of our insides.

"Normal people" enjoy life. Students have a real opportunity when home on vacation, without study pressures, to explore new facets of life with our siblings by sharing with them things they like to do. We Christians often tend to be so tight-lipped and busy with our own important activities that we forget to sit back and laugh and enjoy "playing." I have kept up my skills in water-skiing and snow-skiing, which are expensive in time and money, partly in order to do them with my brother. I'm finding I can enjoy them as God's gifts to me and enjoy my brother and his friends, too.

As we share the activities of our siblings that cause them to blossom, we can see neat new aspects of their personalities. As we appreciate their uniqueness, we can enjoy being with them more, affirm them more, and communicate with them better. The joy and excitement on my brother's face when he has just completed a great ski jump or printed a sharp, clear photograph help me to see what a creative, interesting person he is. Sharing in these things has also helped me to love him and sincerely desire his company. Then I long all the more to bring his talents under the lordship of Christ.

Even if our brother or sister has interests we think are dumb, it's possible to show our respect for him or her as a person by taking time to ask a few questions or going along to observe the project or possession. It's a sure way to communicate the message "I care about you and what goes on in your life." Sometimes it's the beginning of a friendship that has just not been there.

Probably the hardest area in relating to non-Christian siblings is dealing with practices that are plainly wrong. These can range from using drugs to drinking underage, using fake IDs, cheating in school, shoplifting, and on and on. Although I'm still struggling with this, I feel I'm not an appointed judge. The most important thing to be is a friend, not a conscience.

Before I became a Christian I lived in a world I felt had no moral absolute. Therefore I had no reason to do or not do anything, as long as I was willing to pay the consequences. We can relate better to non-Christians if we realize that this might be their world view. We can ask questions to help them understand the legal consequences of their actions and the effect on the people they love. We must not condemn their activities. This does not mean that we condone what they do. However, forcing a lot of rules and morality on non-Christians helps them miss the main issue of God when it comes up. The most important words I have for my brother are those that will lead him to know God's grace in Christ, and I don't want to waste too many on other God-related but secondary issues.

It is here that we can develop the habit of listening with understanding ears. As he tells me something he has done, rather than condemn it, I can ask how he felt about it, how he reacted to the situation, what he liked and didn't like. This helps him think through things for himself and get in touch with his emotions and gut-level reactions. It helps me better understand where he is and what he's going through. He will never tell me all that if he feels judged, so a relaxed atmosphere is vital. Establishing this kind of talking-things-over relationship is necessary in order to communicate anything about the gospel of Christ.

Also necessary for communication of the gospel is continual prayer. We need to pray for our siblings as whole people. This includes their needs and concerns and all aspects of our relationships with them. We also should ask God for sensitivity to openings in conversation, for boldness to pursue conversations and good words to say. We must thank God that he *is* at work in a brother or sister.

It is in this area that I have learned patience in God's working in people's lives. My three years of prayer for my brother have been punctuated with a few good conversations about Christ. Very few—but very good. I have learned to grab every opportunity to communicate that Christianity is not a "Sundays-only, irrelevant religion." In a discussion about Martin Luther King, my brother admitted that he didn't know who Martin Luther was. I mentioned he was one of the men responsible for bringing excitement about the knowledge of Christ back into church music. While the song "Jeremiah Was a Bullfrog" was playing, he questioned the identity of the historical Jeremiah. So I had another opening to drop in a few words about a man whose knowledge of God permeated and encompassed his whole life. Brothers and sisters are often slow to listen to us because we have alienated them in the past by saying too much in a judgmental way. Time does heal, and we can pray and wait and look for fresh opportunities. They will come.

In the past, loyalty, commitment and faithfulness characterized family relationships. That's why the apostle Paul urged that members of the body of Christ be treated as fathers, mothers, brothers and sisters (1 Tim 5:1-2). With such big changes taking place in family stability and structure, we need to mull over the idea of treating family members as we treat members of the Christian "family." We often have patience, real affection and enjoyment of each other as brothers and sisters in Christ. Those relationships took time and at least some self-sacrifice as they grew. Family relationships do too.

Our siblings need to know that we are loyal to them and love them. We must visibly show our commitment to them by setting aside time to spend together on their terms. This often involves sacrificing an activity with a Christian friend. It is always easy to hide our light under the bushel of constant Christian fellowship and to keep all our salt back on campus, far away from home. But we must let the light and salt reach our families. We are selfish (and disobedient to God) if we don't. And it's the best thing we can do for them . . . if we do it with respect and love.

Put Your Dustmop Where Your Mouth Is

by Becky Nessor

10

Ever wonder why it is so hard to witness to those close to us—our family, roommates, or coworkers? I wondered the same thing myself, and it took me one whole summer to figure it out. The problem was my non-Christian parents, or so I thought. I loved them and knew they loved me, but they kept getting on my back, my mom especially.

Somehow they didn't seem all that impressed that I was a Christian. I couldn't figure it out: I had a strong verbal witness for the Lord, and I was always going to church, choir practice and Bible studies. *Surely* they could see I was different.

But Mom did nothing but complain that the house was dirty. We had agreed at the beginning of the summer that it was my job to keep it clean.

The Dusty Trail But my mom's definition of clean and mine were wall-to-wall carpets apart. It wasn't long before she charged that I was not living up to my half of the bargain. I retaliated: "Why do you worry so much about appearances, Mom? People come to visit *us,* not our kitchen sink. After all," I continued, "it's hard enough to find time for housework, what with my job, time to relax, exercise, Inter-Varsity weekends, church, choir practice and small group Bible study—what can you expect?"

Later that day, while cleaning the bathtub, my self-pity grew. "Certainly God wants me involved with other Christians," I reasoned. "Does he expect me to be an immaculate housekeeper, too?"

"No," Jesus seemed to be saying. "The point is not to call attention to your mastery of bathtub ring, but to follow my example."

How often I resolved to follow the Lord's example, as described in Philippians 2:5-11. Somehow the practical application was missing, though the passages before the familiar one are pointed: "Let your everyday life be worthy of the Gospel" (Phil 1:27 Phillips). "Do nothing from selfishness or conceit, but in humility count others better than yourselves. Let each of you look not only to his own interests, but also to the interests of others" (2:3-4).

I suddenly realized the unspoken message to my mom. I had said: "I don't see why spotless is necessary; besides, I hardly have any time for myself." But I had communicated: "I know this is important to you but I don't have time. Therefore, I don't have time for you."

Gulp. I was actually dishonoring the Lord I wanted to proclaim. Did I really expect my mom to believe he is "not a God of confusion but of peace" by the example of my life? Housecleaning skyrocketed up my priority charts when I realized I had been keeping my parents from seeing the good news in action. Rather than dreading the drudgery, I began to look forward to serving my family. I didn't stop the Bible study and church activities. God, who is not bound by time, gave me the hours and energy to live abundantly, which included opening new communication between my parents and me and opening the joy of domestic servanthood to me.

Oops But I still had to watch myself. Plenty of times my witness was more words than deeds, and my mom noticed it. One Sunday evening at church I was one of several to tell how we had accepted Christ. Though my parents weren't with me, they did come to the following Sunday morning service.

A woman introduced herself to my mom and said glowingly, "Your daughter gave such a beautiful testimony last week. She has a wonderful witness for the Lord." Mom looked at me in shock and disgust. *Testimony* and *witness* are among her Top Ten Most Hated Words, right after *death* and *disease.* The woman couldn't have known that. But *I* did, and remembered the times I used high spiritual jargon at home while the coffee table remained undusted. I'm sure my mom must have thought: "All talk, no action."

Everyone has taboos about certain words, subjects or practices. It's easy to stomp on other people by demanding they change their attitudes. But I began to see how much better (and more difficult) it is to be sensitive to my mom, building trust, not walls.

Being a Witness It's actually very easy to witness: we *are* witnesses, as Jesus promised (Acts 1:8). Being a positive witness for him is the issue.

Our habits, manners and lifestyle are the media by which we communicate Christ. My housecleaning, for example, is not the gospel, but it greatly affected my parents' perception of it. The little things—an offhand comment, a neglected courtesy, and in my case, a dirty house—often say much more about our faith than any plan of salvation we may practice.

Guard against compartmentalizing life. The everyday things

may be even more important than all our Bible studies and church socials. Jesus is Lord of all, as Paul indicates: " . . . whatever you do, do all to the glory of God" (1 Cor 10:31). Sometimes we forget to read on to "Give no offense to Jews or Greeks or to the church of God, just as I try to please all men in everything I do, not seeking my own advantage, but that of many, that they may be saved. Be imitators of me, as I am of Christ."

Your Manners Are Showing The effects of nonverbal communication also can be seen in other areas, such as etiquette. Just because Amy Vanderbilt doesn't impress us, must we step on others' toes? People have expectations and feelings, not merely souls to be converted.

Laurie, a leader in our Inter-Varsity chapter, came for a summer weekend. She loved to swim and, because she was a novice water-skier, enjoyed many tows by our speedboat. But during that entire weekend, she never offered to set the table nor wash a dish. She never made her bed but seemed to find time for numerous showers. Just as my mom and I started clearing the table after Sunday dinner, she suddenly decided she "really had to be going" and left. That was over seven years ago and my mother still comments on her. She occasionally adds sarcastically, "that wonderful Christian."

The point is not that Laurie didn't perform certain tasks and fulfill my mother's expectations. She simply was not sensitive to my mother, looking for ways to serve and express her thankfulness. The impression she gave was that she was there to be served and entertained.

Upbringing has a great effect on us but it is the Spirit of the servant Jesus who should control us. Even as a guest, a Christian is to be a servant of love. A servant is alert to be of assistance and comfort to others, expressing gratitude for what he or she has received through words, a written thank-you or, in some situations, a gift.

Are the above suggestions only for our dealings with non-

Christians? Definitely not. Since we *are* witnesses for Christ, all our relationships must be motivated by love. However, we often think "Mike's a Christian; certainly he will understand if I don't phone ahead to say I'll be late" or "I really don't need to straighten up my room—it's only a Bible study."

Jesus said to think more highly of others—any others—than we do of ourselves. He gave clear commands, particularly through apostles James and John, to love the brethren. On the basis of our love for Christians, nonbelievers are given the right to judge two things: whether we truly are Christians and whether Christ was sent from God the Father (Jn 13:35; 17:21).

A Clean Sweep Jesus came to us, taking a particular cultural identity. We are to go out into the world in the same way, being sensitive to other people's ways rather than inadvertently demanding they accommodate themselves to us. We are to minister and communicate on behalf of Christ, who gave himself up for us.

Our lifestyles may be stumbling blocks to others' faith. Our failings give people an excuse not to take the gospel seriously. The world always looks for chances to badmouth the Christian message. As Michael Baughen of London's All Souls' Church says, "We are to grow in grace, so that our lives become less and less an obstacle."

Christians are united by the Spirit of the servant king. By direct teaching and through his example, he told his followers to "spend and be spent" for others. For the habitually messy, this means refusing to say "that's just the way I am" but instead sharing the workload to serve others. For the cleanaholic, this means cleaning not for one's own ego but for others' needs. For the untactful, sensitivity means guarding against outshouting all their good intentions.

For everyone, the goal is to be doers of the Word, not speakers only.

Becky Nessor has a B.A. in journalism and lives in Illinois.

Part 3
Coping with Problems

My Parents Are Impossible

by Walter Trobisch

11

After reading *I Loved a Girl* by Walter Trobisch, a young African teacher named Elsie began corresponding with the author who was at that time a missionary in Africa. The following is an excerpt from *My Parents Are Impossible* (IVP), the chronicle of their letters first published in HIS as "My Father Is Impossible." She asked for and received the author's permission to address him as Father.

December 6th

Dear Father,

I am stuck. My father cannot approve of my choice of a husband. He says that all men of Dick's tribe are unfaithful to their wives and that he has heard rumors that Dick misbehaved at college.

However, I can tell you that since I have known him, he has

never shown me any nonsense. In both of our tribes there is a high appreciation of virginity and Dick fully accepts my decision on this point. In this respect I have remained "African" even when I was in Europe.

It is at another point that I come into conflict with our African tradition. We were brought up in strict obedience to our parents. Also the divine commandment says, "Thou shalt honor thy father and mother that it may be well with thee and thou mayest live long on earth."

I looked up Martin Luther's explanation of this commandment. He says, "We should so fear and love God that we do not despise our parents and superiors, nor provoke them to anger, but honor, serve, obey, love and esteem them."

Tell me, is there an exception to this commandment? Do we always have to obey our parents?

Sincerely,
(Miss) Elsie S.K.

December 25th

Dear Elsie,

Sorry for the delay, but I didn't find time before Christmas to answer your last letter. It makes me sad to hear that your father does not accept Dick. "Honor your parents" means first of all in this case to try to understand them.

You see, your parents have always lived within their own tribe. They never had a chance to get closely acquainted with people of different tribes. For them an intertribal marriage was something unheard of.

When they sent you to high school and later on to college you grew up with boys and girls from different tribes. You saw their differences, but you also realized that they are not so terribly different after all. You met them as persons. Your parents have never had this experience.

True, there are certain difficulties in an intertribal marriage.

Differences in customs and preferences could create barriers. But I don't think that they are insurmountable. They can be overcome by mutual love and understanding, at least much more easily than if you had different religions or belonged to different cultures.

I feel you should also understand each other's mother tongue. This is not only important for a good relationship with the in-laws, but also for the relationship between Dick and you. English will remain for both of you a foreign tongue. One likes to express the innermost feelings of the heart in one's own mother tongue. It is indispensable for your marriage to be able to express such feelings.

Now you see where generalizations and prejudices lead to! As you once said to me about the old people—"they are all stupid fools"—so your father says about the men of Dick's tribe that "they are all unfaithful to their wives." Just as you didn't take time to reason with the old people, so your father doesn't take time to reason with you, but rather believes this slander about Dick.

Elsie, I see only one way out. "Honor, serve, love and esteem your parents" means in your case that you take Dick to your father so that he can meet him as a person. I am sure that if the two men have looked into each other's eyes and if your father sees how much you love Dick, things will start to change.

I am enclosing a letter which I have written to your father. Read it first and if you think it is all right, give it to him. I hope it will help to change his attitude.

Yes, there is an exception to the commandment of obedience to our parents. It is indicated in Acts 5:29, "We must obey God rather than men." If our parents demand that we act against God's will, we must disobey them.

But we never should do that lightheartedly and never before having tried everything possible to reach an agreement. Even if we are forced to disobey our parents we should never "despise them" or "provoke them to anger" but rather avoid everything that could hurt them. We must show them every sign of love and esteem in spite of their opposition.

Remember, you have a heavenly Father who is more real and closer to you than any earthly father could be. Earthly fathers are only poor substitutes, thin shadows and dim reflections of this heavenly Father, who loves you and accepts you even when the earthly fathers fail.

Why not open your Bible when lonesome times come and ask your heavenly Father to talk to you in a very personal way?

I hope and pray that your heavenly Father may also talk to your earthly father through the enclosed letter.

Christmas Day

Dear brother in Christ,

For a long time I have debated with myself whether I should write you this letter. But after nine months of correspondence with your daughter, Elsie, I feel I should do it. I am asking you to see in me not only a fellow Christian, but also a fellow father. I write to you on Christmas Day when our heavenly Father sent us his Son in order to make us his children.

Elsie told me that you disapprove of her choice of Richard because he belongs to another tribe. I can imagine that you grew up with a feeling of hostility toward this tribe. But, you see, such feelings do not exist for Elsie. Members of this tribe were her classmates and became her friends. There is no barrier any more between her and them.

But, dear brother, isn't this a hopeful sign? Isn't Africa sick of tribalism? Isn't it hindering the building up of the African nations and the cooperation between these nations? Isn't it even dividing the churches in Africa?

Therefore, I feel we should be happy if these barriers break down. We as Christians should be the first ones to lay aside prejudice and hostility.

Many African young people who are considering an intertribal marriage have written to me. They all complain that they run up against a wall of nonunderstanding and silence on the part of their parents. I am afraid that the older generation is loading upon itself a great amount of guilt here and I must remind you of the apostle's warning: "Fathers, do not provoke your children to anger" (Eph 6:4).

I have advised Elsie to take Dick home with her once and to introduce him to you. Please receive him well. Forget that he belongs to another tribe and meet him as the young man whom your daughter loves.

It is my definite impression, as far as I can judge from a distance, that there is genuine love between both of them. One sign of it is that Richard respects your daughter's moral convictions and her personality as a woman. He has asked for her hand in marriage and has promised to be faithful to her his whole life. So he did not, as so many do, demand the surrender of her body without making possible the surrender of her soul.

Furthermore, Elsie and Dick have gotten acquainted with each other as they worked together as teachers. All teachers are in a way prolonged and specialized fathers and mothers to their students. Elsie and Dick have taken this task of teaching very conscientiously. I don't know of any better preparation for marriage. At least, I am sure, they know a hundred times more about each other than those who try to gain this knowledge by premarital sex. As a father, I would be most happy if my daughter submitted her love to such a foolproof test.

Let me mention another point. As a father, you are the first "man" whom your daughter meets. Unless this relationship is warmhearted and healthy, it will be difficult for her to establish a healthy relationship with other men. Girls with "cold fathers" tend to become "old maids," hostile to all men, or if they marry, often they become frigid wives who are unable to respond fully to the tenderness of their husbands.

Therefore the importance of the relationship between a daughter and her father cannot be overestimated. You hold the key to her future happiness in your hands when you take time to listen and talk to her when she is home and to correspond with her when she is away. Yes, you should even offer her once in a while a bit of physical tenderness, embrace her when she comes home or goes away, stroke her hair when she is sad or sit at her bedside when she is sick.

In this way you can protect your daughter from many errors and give her the best help in her most intimate problems. Many girls do not get into trouble because they are sexually greedy, but because they are starved for tenderness.

Don't be afraid that you will lose your authority in this way. Many fathers think that they can only keep their authority by ruling as distant patriarchs, but in this way they reveal their own insecurity. The real reason why so few fathers talk to their daughters is that deep down in their hearts they are afraid of them.

It's only a small step from the patriarch to the dictator and tyrant. The tyrant rules by spreading fear because he is a victim of fear himself.

Africa is sick of patriarchalism. Africa needs not patriarchs, but fathers, true fathers who reflect by their loving-kindness and nearness to their children, the nearness and loving-kindness of our heavenly Father.

I hope and pray, dear brother, that this letter may help you to become closer to Elsie and make you more grateful to your heavenly Father for having made you the father of such a wonderful daughter as Elsie. You can be proud of her.

January 18

Dear Father,

My parents have become impossible.

I followed your advice and went to my home village with Dick. But my father didn't even want to see me, let alone Dick.

I asked mother whether I should show your letter to father, but she discouraged me. She was afraid father would think that I have accused him in Europe of being a dictator and tyrant.

My younger brother is on my side, but unfortunately he was not at home. Only my older brother was home. He wants me to marry one of his ex-schoolmates who is studying at present in the United States, but I am not interested in him.

They expect him to return soon and are corresponding with him secretly. I tried my best to get those letters, but I failed. I am beginning to lose confidence in my family.

I tell you, when the fool comes from America, I am ready for him. I am going to teach him a lesson he will never forget. I shall not refuse to go with him to his house, but there I shall destroy and break everything that comes in my hands. When he reports it to the police, I shall accuse him of kidnapping me.

Father, I am rather stranded. I wish to get your advice. Do you understand my situation?

I feel like doing something that could hurt my father. If he is not willing to listen to my plea, he is going to regret it. I am going to be a castaway. I have decided to remain single for the rest of my life, unless I can marry Dick.

Tell me, is it possible for a girl to live her life without marriage? I see so many unhappy marriages in my vicinity that I am almost afraid to get married. Still I would like to become a mother. I could imagine my life without a husband, but not without a baby.

This letter of Elsie's reminded me of the child who was bitten by a snake and said: "This is the right punishment for my father. Why didn't he give me any shoes?"

Elsie wants to punish her father by remaining single, a state which—interestingly enough—she compares with a "castaway." I don't know how serious she is, but she must know how she can hurt her father best.

He certainly has succeeded now to "provoke his child to anger." But just her anger reveals her attachment to him. The opposite of love is not hatred, but indifference. As long as she hates him, she still is not indifferent to him.

What strikes me is that here again—as in my correspondence with Cecile in my book I Loved a Girl—*I run up against the wall which separates father and daughter. I am at a loss as to how to break it down. Neither Cecile nor Elsie could talk to their fathers. Cecile was hardly able to write to hers; Elsie could not even give him a letter from me.*

The thought comes to me that one of the deepest reasons why Elsie sees so many unhappy marriages in her vicinity is that the young women have no relationship with their fathers. As married wives they do not expect any personal relationship with their husbands who in turn are not prepared to give something which is not expected. When these fathers have daughters themselves, they establish the same nonrelationship with them and thus plant in them the seeds of death for their future marriages.

What would happen to marriages in Africa—and maybe in the whole world—if women had fatherly fathers?

This is how I answered Elsie:

January 28

Dear "Daughter" Elsie,

Your letter made me very sad.

How can these poor and helpless fathers ever change if nobody talks to them and tells them what is wrong with them? Why didn't you just run after your father and hug him when he did not want to talk to you?

You were so eager to give Cecile advice about talking to her father, but you yourself are not even able to hand over a letter to him from me! I am sorry that you didn't. Though I can understand your reasoning, I would have been so curious about his reaction. I don't think it could have made things worse.

When the "fool" comes, please talk to him quietly first. Don't make him an enemy unless you have to. This man may have some thoughts of his own and you may even be able to win him to your side. Maybe if he would plead for Dick, your father would listen and you would not have to remain single after all.

This is only a possibility, of course. More and more African women are able to earn their livelihood as teachers, nurses or secretaries and thus become financially independent and able to exist without being married.

It is possible, Elsie, but it is certainly not easy. Even in Western society, in spite of the emancipation of women and all the talk about it, single women are still treated in many ways as "cast-aways" and in Africa this will probably be true for a long time. Traditional African society did not provide a place for unmarried women and this attitude will not change overnight.

If you remain single voluntarily, at least you must know why. It's the motive which counts. The reasons you give are not valid because they are negative.

If you remain single in a sulky attitude, just out of stubbornness, in order to spite your father and to hurt him, you will not be able to master the problems of single life and you certainly are not guided by God.

Those who choose voluntarily not to marry for negative reasons become "old maids" or—prostitutes. This is what the prostitute and the old maid have in common: They both have a negative relationship with men.

There are positive reasons not to marry. For instance, God could guide you to remain single because as a single teacher you would have more time for your students and could be a better "mother" to them. This would be a valid reason. But you must be very sure about this special personal guidance. If God calls you to this life, you could develop to full womanhood or even "motherhood."

I know a nurse in a remote bush hospital who broke her engagement in order to give herself completely to the task of caring for her patients. She is actually "married" to this task and very happy.

This happiness, however, includes the sacrifice of two things: sex and her own children. It is not motherhood that you have to renounce but having your own children. The right of a child to have its own father is much more important than your desire to have your own baby.

However, in your case, dear Elsie, I have a big question mark in my mind as to whether it is God's will that you remain single. To me it looks as if you would flee into the single state as others flee into marriage.

In your first letter you wrote to me, "If my father tries to sell me, I shall disobey him." Why don't you disobey now? Isn't there any way to get married in your country without your parents' consent?

P.S. I would like to ask a favor of you. Our correspondence has touched so many problems which are the problems of hundreds, maybe even thousands. Would you allow me to publish our correspondence in part, without mentioning your name, of course?

February 16

Dear Rev. T.,

Yes, you may publish from our correspondence whatever you feel is profitable for others as long as you do not mention my name and reveal my country. I do not want to claim your letters only for myself.

Please do not think that I am not thankful for them even if I ask you today not to write to me anymore.

Yes, there is a way to get legally married in my country without the parents' consent. I would estimate that about ten per cent of the married couples have eloped and married at the magistrate court. Twenty-five per cent of the women have children out of wedlock, because their parents did not approve of their choice of a partner.

However, if you marry against the will of your parents, the quarrels with the families will not end. They will not only create trouble but will also claim that all the troubles that occur to you are punishment for your disobedience. If you need help they will refuse it.

As far as I am concerned I am not at peace to marry against the will of my father. In fact, I wouldn't be able to do it.

I am not going to be long today. It is not necessary to trouble you. I feel tired of what I have been facing and I want to speak of it no more.

You note the change of address. Please do not ask me any questions.

One thing has happened though, through our correspondence: I have found a new relationship to my heavenly Father of whom you once said, "He loves me and accepts me even when the earthly father fails." I can believe this now. I have started to read my Bible regularly and I can pray as I never did before.

Please do not answer. I'll see the way out.

Goodbye to you and your good family

from Elsie

Just as the counselor has to be ready when the other one wants to speak, so he too has to respect the other's desire to remain silent.

I never heard from Elsie again. Did she remain single? Did she marry Dick? Or someone else? Did she actually become an embittered "old maid"? I don't know.

But one thing I know: The silence between the generations is lethal, as lethal as the silence between Elsie and her father. It is the counterpart of patriarchalism and stands among Africa's greatest enemies.

That lethal silence turned a young woman, full of energy, good will and constructive ideas, intelligent and gifted, on her way to womanhood and motherhood, into a frustrated and powerless cripple fed up with life.

Elsie is a victim of the conflict between old and new. Her head was in the future, but her heart lived still in the past. With her thinking she protested and rebelled. With her feelings she sub-

mitted and obeyed.

But I am afraid this submission and obedience destroyed her life—just as her disobedience would have done, for by disobeying the patriarch she would have sacrificed the father.

Africa's problem of today is that, as patriarchalism breaks down, the patriarchs are not as yet being replaced by fathers. The destruction of an authoritarian patriarchalism is in itself no solution unless true fatherliness takes its place.

Is it only an African problem? Is it not a world problem?

Isn't the unrest among young people all over the world today a rebellion against the false authority of patriarchalism and at the same time an expression of a deep longing for the true authority of fatherliness?

If this is the case, we are facing here not a social or political problem but in the first place a religious one. Wherever fatherliness and true authority occur on this earth, they are a gift from our heavenly Father, a grace, a reflection of his image.

Patriarchalism is a sign that this image was lost.

It is not true that we create an image of God according to the image we have of our earthly fathers. On the contrary, he conveys his image to us and gives everything which is called "father" on this earth his imprint (Eph 3:14-15).

This alone makes us fathers. More than that—it makes us men. Fatherliness is an integral part of manhood. Because Elsie's father did not mature to full manhood, he could not help her to full womanhood.

Fatherliness does not necessarily mean to have children of one's own. Fatherly men can become spiritual fathers, as many of my Roman Catholic colleagues have proven themselves to be and as I tried to become for Elsie, at least for a period of her life.

In her last letter she addressed me again as Rev. T. I must admit that at first this hurt me a little, but I was comforted when she said, "I pray to my heavenly Father, who loves me and accepts me when the earthly father fails."

I take it as a sign that I served as a bridge and that she threw herself completely into his arms.

I know that he will be a better counselor to her than I was. He alone can "turn the heart of the fathers to the children and the heart of the children to their fathers" as it is promised in the last verse of the Old Testament opening up the way to the New.

Walter Trobisch, until his death in 1979, lived with his wife, Ingrid, in Austria, where they carried on a vital counseling service by mail. Their marriage ministry, Family Life Mission, also took them on lecture tours around the world. Among his most popular books are Love Is a Feeling to Be Learned, I Married You *(Harper & Row), and* Love Yourself.

My Dad Drinks Too Much

by Arthur Hunt

12

That day was worse than usual. Dad drank beer most of the day, but in between beers he took large quantities of vodka. I usually stayed in my room and avoided him when he drank like that—stayed away from the inevitable conflicts it caused.

I was a twenty-one-year-old college student at the time. Although I'd committed my life to Jesus three years earlier, I still didn't like to be around Dad when he was drunk, and the smell of liquor made me sick. I was thankful that my mom was in Texas visiting relatives; my sister and two of my brothers were gone too. Only twenty-three-year-old Dave was home. Dave had recently returned from an Army assignment in Europe. While he was there, his relationship with Jesus had gotten knocked out of him. He came back incredibly mixed up and confused.

I was worried because he was home that night. He and Dad had always had an intense love-hate relationship. They both wanted to show love to each other, but they were too much alike —bull-headed and stubborn. Dad made Dave feel like a failure, and Dave had little respect for Dad. No matter what Dad asked him to do, Dave would find a way to disobey. Sometimes I thought they were both like little children.

If one of them would have accepted the other for what he was, they could have had a great love between them, even in the midst of all their problems. They both craved affection.

Clash and Conflict It was getting late and Dad was hardly able to speak. I had watched him drink for so many years that I knew the stages he passed through. When he'd get drunk on beer he'd just become loud and eventually fall asleep. But vodka put a crazy look in his eyes. He would get mean and everything that came out of his mouth was filthy. I went into the kitchen to get something to drink. I'll never forget the revulsion I felt for my dad as he sat there destroying himself. I knew it was wrong for me to feel that way, and I prayed about it. Somehow God softened my heart, and I sat down and began to talk to the lonely man who was my father.

Everything was fine until Dave came in. I could tell right away that I'd better try to steer the conversation so that he wouldn't get into an argument. Dave was obviously disgusted with Dad. He made one subtle slur and Dad bristled. They began to argue. I tried to calm them down, but the argument gained momentum. Their anger was building, and there was nothing I could do about it.

Dad, caught up in the argument and the booze, lashed out at Dave and said, "You're nothing but a damn failure." Then something happened to Dave that I had never seen before. His body tensed and his eyes enlarged. It was as if all the years of being hurt had added up. His hand shot out, knocking the beer and other things off the table. He grabbed Dad, pushed him off his chair and said with absolute bitterness, "I hate you."

I helped Dad up, then tried to get Dave out of the room. But when Dave pushed him, Dad popped too. They were both beyond reason. Dad was yelling at the top of his voice, "No kid of mine is going to hit me in my own house! You'd better get out of here or I'm going to blow your head off!" This made Dave even madder, and he shoved Dad against the wall, telling him he wasn't leaving. He started to walk away and Dad headed for his own bedroom.

"I'll fix you!" Dad yelled.

Nightmare I went into Dad's room and found him trying to load his shotgun. He was so drunk he was having a hard time doing it. While I was trying to get the gun away from him, Dave came in and saw the gun.

"You'd shoot your own son?" Dave yelled. And then he came at Dad. He grabbed for the gun and they struggled briefly. During the scuffle the shotgun struck the large bedroom windows and smashed them to bits. Glass flew everywhere. Finally Dave got the gun and removed the shells. The two began to wrestle, Dave crying even while he was fighting. As he hit Dad he yelled, "You never loved me, did you? You never loved me!" He repeated it over and over.

Frantically I tried to come between them. When I got them apart Dave told Dad that he was leaving the house and not coming back. Dad was furious. As Dave went out the front door to his car, Dad followed him, yelling obscenities. Dave turned around. They met in the middle of the yard, fighting and yelling. I got down with them, still trying to break up the fight, as they rolled around on the wet ground in the dark. But Dave had a forty-pound advantage over me. It was impossible. Finally, after both of them were bleeding and drained of energy, Dad got away and went inside the house. Dave just sat there on the lawn, staring. At last he got up slowly and walked away.

I just stood gazing up at the sky, shaking, crying and praying. I had prayed for my dad ever since I had become a Christian—for three long years. And there I was, staring up into a dark sky with my lonely prayers unanswered. I had never felt so powerless and empty. And alone.

Close to Home Perhaps this scene is all too familiar to you. One or both of your parents drink and, as a result, you suffer—mentally, spiritually and perhaps even physically. Maybe you've had that same feeling of utter loneliness and despair—the hopelessness that comes from not knowing what to do.

Some of my earliest memories are of my father coming home drunk and arguing with my mother. I always wanted to love Dad, but I grew up hiding from him because of his drinking. When I became a Christian, I had to make a choice. Either I could go on hiding, allowing the bitterness I felt to eat away at me, or I could ask God to change my attitude and help me to cope with the father he had given me. God helped me learn to relate to my father. He can help you also, and make your time at home something better than it is now.

The following suggestions are not cure-alls. Each situation is different. My father, for example, always provided for us even in the midst of his problem. And when he wasn't drinking, he was as nice as anyone. Your situation may be more severe or less so, but if you apply some scriptural principles in relating to the parent who has a drinking problem, you will find that God can work in you to bring about a solution.

Clean Slate First, *have a clear conscience* toward your parent who drinks. Only someone who has had a family member with a drinking problem knows the bitterness that can grow from being repeatedly hurt. You want to love, but a hate grows in you that seems uncontrollable. You may think the person is not aware of how you feel. You're wrong. He or she perceives your attitude; you can never hide emotions as strong as disgust and bitterness.

In 1 Timothy 1:18-19 Paul says, "I . . . sent you out to battle for the right armed only with your faith and a clear conscience. Some, alas, have laid these simple weapons contemptuously aside and, as far as their faith is concerned, have run their ships on the rocks" (Phillips). Paul is telling Timothy that, next to his faith, a clear conscience is his most essential weapon. Bill Gothard defines a clear conscience as the freedom of spirit and assurance that come from knowing that you are transparent toward everyone, that no one is able to accuse you of wrongs that you have never made right with him. These wrongs could be any number of things, but one of the easiest ways to wrong a parent who drinks is by being bitter toward him or her.

Hebrews 12:14-15 talks about a "root of bitterness" that can spring up, causing deep trouble. If you have been guilty of bitterness, you need to confess it, first to God and then to the one whom you have offended. Only in this way can you gain a clear conscience.

Begin to Love Clearing your conscience toward parents who drink will help you find love toward them. In 1 Timothy 1:5 we see that "the aim of our charge is love that issues from a pure heart and a good conscience and sincere faith." This Scripture clearly indicates that there is a connection between love and a good conscience. If you really want to begin to love the one who drinks, a clear conscience toward him or her could be the first step.

Assess your attitudes, figure out where you have wronged the person, and ask him or her for forgiveness. I have found that saying "I'm sorry" is too easy. Instead, say something like: "Dad [or Mom], I realize that I have wronged you by being bitter toward you. Will you forgive me?"

I'll never forget the time I went to my dad, not long after I had become a Christian, and asked him to forgive me for a whole list of things. I picked a time when he wasn't drinking. He was in a good mood, and we were sitting together talking. When I asked him to forgive me, he put his head down trying to hide his tears, and said he forgave me. That was a turning point in our relationship. From then on I could tell him exactly what was on my mind because he knew I was speaking with the right motives. Our honesty grew. Many times after that we sat at the kitchen table and talked.

Your parent may not react like mine. He or she may yell you out of the room—or shun you in silence. But it's important for you to take the initiative, to clear your own conscience and open the door to your parent's response.

Another benefit of asking my dad's forgiveness was that a new kind of love began to develop once I stopped harboring wrong feelings toward him. It was a long process because he was still drinking, still hurting me and other members of my family. But it was a start.

Pure Witness Another reason to gain a clear conscience toward a parent who drinks is the effect on our witness: "In your hearts reverence Christ as Lord. Always be prepared to make a defense to any one who calls you to account for the hope that is in you, yet do it with gentleness and reverence, and keep your conscience clear, so that, when you are abused, those who revile your good behavior in Christ may be put to shame" (1 Pet 3:15-16).

If you have wronged your parents, they will feel justified in ignoring your message. If your parents who drink feel, for example, that you have a spirit of bitterness toward them, you are hurting your Christian witness immeasurably. But if you have cleared your conscience toward them, they will be "ashamed" when they falsely accuse you. The Holy Spirit will have a clearer channel to communicate to them.

Forgiveness Second, *forgive from your heart.* When I went in and asked my dad to forgive me, I half expected him to say, "No, it's *I* who should ask *you* to forgive *me.*" But he didn't. His eyes were blinded. He didn't know how much he had hurt me through the years. He didn't ask me to forgive him. But I forgave him anyway.

In Mark 11:25, Jesus gives the sobering command, "And

whenever you stand praying, forgive, if you have anything against any one; so that your Father also who is in heaven may forgive you your trespasses." God expects us to forgive those who wrong us even if they never ask for forgiveness. It's not easy. But it's worth it.

Why is it so hard to forgive? One reason is that withholding forgiveness is a kind of punishment. It's our way of getting back at the one we feel has wronged us. But we must have the mind of Christ. He suffered for us. It wasn't fair for him to be crucified; he had done nothing. Yet he suffered for you and me because he loved us. Even while he was dying, he forgave the people who were crucifying him and asked the Father to do the same.

Forgiving may not seem fair from a human viewpoint, but it is God's higher way. A great release comes with forgiveness. Instead of thinking about how someone has wronged you, and getting tighter and tighter inside, you can begin to thank God for that person. Forgiveness cleanses you. Obviously, as human beings we do not forgive perfectly. We sometimes slip and begin to feel sorry for ourselves, blaming it on the one who is drinking. Although I felt no hate toward my dad when he fought with Dave, I had an overwhelming temptation to condemn him. I fought against it. God can help you separate the sin from the sinner. When God looks on us, he doesn't turn away in disgust because we are sinners. He hates the sin, but he loves the sinner. We should do the same.

One important caution: Do not confuse forgiveness and indifference. They are not the same. Because you don't want to have the wrong feelings, you may decide to have *no* feelings. An icy hardness may creep into your life. Let God give you an open, forgiving heart. Sometimes you will fail. But don't give up.

The Fifth Commandment Third, *honor your father and mother.* It is easy for the children of alcoholics to cop out on this commandment. Ephesians 6:1-3 says: "Children, obey your parents in the Lord, for this is right. 'Honor your father and mother' (this is the first commandment with a promise), 'that it may be well with you and that you may live long on the earth.' "

When a parent has a drinking problem, it is sometimes very hard to give him or her honor. Remember that the person usually has a very low self-image. There is little self-respect even though the person may *sound* like an egotist. What he or she needs and wants is to be treated with respect, to be told, "You are important." After I learned this principle, I tried to think of ways to honor my father. Once, when I needed advice on a college matter, I went to him and asked his opinion. His chest swelled. The bond between us grew. I was honoring him. I sincerely wanted his opinion and he appreciated it.

But honoring is not simply buttering up your parents. It is a basic attitude that includes obedience. If you are still living at home you are under their authority and therefore subject to them. In the past you may have had so little respect for your parent who drinks that you were unwilling to obey him or her, or if you did, you were sullen. But God expects us to obey our parents. Having a parent who drinks doesn't change the scriptural principle. (Of course, if your parent asks you to do something that goes against a scriptural principle, God's law has more authority.)

Even if you are living away from home, honoring your parents can still involve deference to them. Don't let their drinking be an excuse for you to sin. Don't withhold obedience from your parents because they drink. Strive to develop respect for them. If you have followed the first two steps—gaining a clear conscience and forgiving from your heart—you'll find it easier to give the honor that your parents so desperately want and need.

God can and will forgive you any sins you have committed. But it is important not to feel false guilt for your parent's condition. Alcoholics often blame others and try to convince them that they are "driving them to drink." Don't let Satan falsely accuse you. You are not responsible for the problem. Ask God to free you from this burden of false guilt.

Don't Give Up Fourth, *keep praying*. Pray for your family. Pray that God will make you a peacemaker in the family. Ask him to make you an example and give you encouragement. Most of all, pray that God will save your parent who drinks. He says in his Word that it is not his will that any should perish, but that *all* should reach repentance. God's will for your parent is that he or she will be born again and begin a new life. Never, never give up praying for that.

Frankly, at times when I was praying for my father, I did give up hope. I was praying with little faith. But I *was* praying. Eventually, God supplied the faith.

After that terrible night with Dave, things got worse at our house. My parents separated; Dad drank more and more. I thought things might never change, but I was wrong—God showed me what he could do. Two years after the incident, my dad received Jesus into his life. He was born again.

Like many others, my dad had had to sink as low as he could before realizing what bad shape his life was in. He had lost his wife and his job, and he was on a binge when a horrible hallucination scared him enough to let God get through to him. For once he listened, and God came into his life.

After his encounter with God, my dad's drinking problem seemed to disappear. But those of us who love him regret now that he didn't seek treatment and counseling for alcoholism even after he was saved. Without counseling, he has had recurrent bouts with the problem. He thought that because he was a Christian, he could take a beer once in a while without being affected. Nothing could have been further from the truth.

I've learned that many who have a genuine rebirth still have a problem with alcohol. The good news is that your parent who drinks will now be more motivated to change. Demonstrating a desire to conquer the problem is the first step in controlling alcoholism once and for all. Urge your parent to see a good Christian counselor as soon as possible after he or she is saved.

Some of you are still in the midst of a problem with no end

in sight. Remember, there is always hope. I prayed for my dad for five years before he was saved. No matter how bad things seem, no matter how much a person drinks, there is hope. Keep praying.

I know that it's not easy to live with a parent who drinks. It is difficult to have the right attitude, difficult to love, difficult to forgive. But I've also discovered that God honors our attempts to follow him—to follow his example of forgiveness and love.

Arthur Hunt is a pastor in Parkdale, Oregon.

When My Parents Split Up

A HIS Panel Discussion

13

Everyone has friends who are victims of family breakups. Perhaps you are a victim yourself. Many have not sorted themselves out since their parents' divorce, even if it was many years before. Many refuse to talk about the divorce with anyone else. In an attempt to encourage those with deep hurts to share their burdens with others, HIS magazine talked with four students whose parents have divorced. All names are fictitious.

How did you feel at the time of your parents' divorce?

Steve: I'd been anticipating it for some time. When I found out what had been going on for twenty-five or twenty-six years, and that my parents had kept it hushed up for all that time, I felt sort of relieved that my mom was let out of such a tense situation.

I felt bitter toward my father afterward, and partially still do. I felt betrayed when I found out that he had been sleeping around for fifteen years. It really hurt to think he had been putting on a show.

Darlene: I was nine when my parents got divorced and I don't think I even knew what the word really meant. When my dad left home, it was just unbelievable to me. It's hard to remember whether I felt bitter or angry. I know I bawled my head off.

And I never believed it was forever. I always thought my dad would come back home. I prayed each night that he would come back. I wrote him letters. I always felt that he would return. Four years later when he remarried, I knew he would never return. I was old enough then to realize that divorce was permanent. Now I've come to accept it.

Rob: I was twelve. I didn't really know what was going on between my parents until right at the end when it became obvious that something was wrong. I remember when my dad told me that they were going to separate and eventually get a divorce. I was really crushed and hurt over the idea. Whatever emotion I had was in that day or two when I first heard about it.

Then I decided that if that's the way they're going to be, then I'm not going to let it ruin my life. So I sort of forgave them and went on my way, taking each day as it came.

Judy: I was twelve also, and the divorce was a total shock. We kids never heard fighting or anything until the night they called the lawyer. I was completely shocked.

My way of dealing with it was to not deal with it at all—I just suppressed my emotions. I didn't cry when my mother left. I just got sort of sick to my stomach. For almost eight years I hid my feelings. I never talked about my real feelings about the divorce to anyone. I just acted as though it had no effect on me at all.

Since I was the oldest child, I played mother of the family for a few years (we stayed with my dad, who later remarried). I took care of everybody, did the cooking and cleaning, and had to be strong. But deep inside I felt abandoned and insecure.

I suppressed these feelings until I was a sophomore in college. My father was going through his second divorce, and all the same feelings came up again. But this time they all came out, even though I was seven hundred miles from home.

I went into a deep depression at school and couldn't concentrate on my studies. I was flunking one of my courses, and my skin kept breaking out in an itchy rash that wouldn't clear up. I was moody and withdrawn. My boyfriend couldn't figure out what was wrong with me, and neither could I. I talked to a couple of teachers at school, but they just said my problem was that I was in love. At first I had no idea that this depression and confusion was linked to that first divorce; I just had this vague feeling of being in the pits.

How have you related to the parent who left and the parent you stayed with?

Darlene: When my dad left, I tried to relate to him the same as before, but gradually we just saw each other on weekends. Then when he remarried, I blocked him out completely. I wouldn't visit him anymore. I didn't go to his wedding. I didn't acknowledge that his wife existed. I wouldn't talk to her. I just blocked him out of my mind.

On the other hand, I accepted every word my mother said about my father as absolutely true. But I wouldn't believe his word, especially when it conflicted with Mom's. I always heard differing stories about things, like how much money we have and who's paying for my education. My mom would say, in effect, "Darlene, I work so hard to put food on the table and your father doesn't do *anything*. He doesn't have any part in your upbringing."

Well, yes, Dad wasn't there to rear us, but he did provide money every single month. Still I believed everything my mother said. It took one hard weekend for me to realize what I had done when my father confronted me about it only a couple of years ago. It was an intense time, but a turning point for me. After that weekend, gradually I was able to love and accept him as a person and as my father.

Steve: I felt very bitter toward my father. My parents separated about five months before the divorce, and he went to live with this woman he'd been going out with for a while.

I was so mad that one day I got in my car and drove forty miles to where he was living. I sat in the car outside his apartment building for about three hours, just waiting for him to pull up. I was really going to let him have it with both barrels. Maybe it was good for both of us that he didn't show up.

My mom never made us take sides. That's something I'll always thank her for. She never badmouthed my father to us. But I still blame my father pretty much, and he blames himself. I know it's not one hundred per cent one person's fault that the marriage broke up. But it's still easy to put the bulk of the blame on my father.

Darlene: Neither of my parents were Christians when they got married. They were having problems about eleven or twelve years into the marriage—probably earlier than that. My mom went to see a pastor and he led her to the Lord.

At about the same time Mom became a Christian, Dad left. So I figured he left because she became a Christian. I really blamed him for it, because I couldn't understand why he would leave her just because she believed in God and went to church on Sunday. (I wasn't a Christian at this time, and I didn't understand religion at all.)

It wasn't until years later that I understood there had to be more problems than just her belief in God. A marriage takes two people. Even though one partner can mess it up, I think both people play a part in any divorce.

Judy: My parents' problem—and our whole family's—was communication. We never communicated about *anything* other than superficial things. When Mom walked out the door I never even said, "I'm going to miss you." We kept our feelings below the surface.

Rob: I would put most of the blame on my father. He had been running around for quite a while before the divorce. I know my mom tried to communicate with him, but it was hard. She had strong feelings about some things, and I'm sure she caused some of the conflict.

As the divorce went through court Dad gave Mom a very hard time. There were verbal battles and awful episodes of backbiting between them. I couldn't help but feel lots of animosity toward my dad.

Also, Dad had a bad temper, and he turned it on us kids at times. When you're twelve years old and your dad tells you you're no good and calls you worthless, something inside of you snaps and you have to stand up and say, "But I *do* have some worth; there *is* some good in me."

My mom was very good about it. She tried not to make us choose one way or the other, but her resentments toward my father naturally came out and we kids picked them up.

But I still felt a natural love for my father and wanted to have respect for him. Over the years I've tried to see the good and the bad things in him, yet encourage the role that I think he should play. And gradually he has begun to take more of an active role in my life.

Judy: I agree with you, Rob, about respecting your parents *and* respecting yourself. There are ways in which I think I've outgrown my parents. At first I tended to look down on them and say, "Why can't you be adults? Why do I always have to be the adult?"

But also there's something to honoring them as people and parents that makes a real difference in our relationship. After I had released my initial feelings and after I became a Christian, I realized that God can give me the strength and the ability to understand and honor my parents.

Steve: That's my problem right now. My father doesn't want to be reached. Not that he doesn't feel love for us, but he really feels he's failed as a father and a husband. I think that's why he won't get in touch with us.

Both of my parents are remarried. My mom married a man who is totally the opposite of my father—he gives her love and attention and makes us feel welcome into his family. So I feel a conflict in myself between the strong character of my stepfather and the weak character of my father. My father knows his weaknesses. I've talked with him a couple of times about them, and I can tell it hurts him. He feels that my mom's new husband is everything he was not.

My father is remarried to a woman about my age. I haven't met her yet—that's going to be a little rough. He knows that he married the person who was the cause of the divorce. Even though he's not a Christian as far as I know, he does feel a tremendous amount of guilt. It seems that no amount of reassurance from my brother, my sister or myself is going to help much.

Rob: My father's not a Christian either. I don't know if he would *say* he feels guilty for what happened, but I think he does feel guilt, even though it may not be conscious. I'm sure he feels guilty because the relationships among the family members are not right. And it shows whenever I get together with him because he knows that when problems in the past are not dealt with they hurt our present communication. I think his guilt has stayed with him through the years because he hasn't dealt with it.

How do you get along with your stepparents?

Judy: I've felt very resentful toward them over the years. In fact, just this past year I'm finally able to accept my mother's husband as a person. I started out ten years ago by just blindly accepting him because he was married to my mom. Then I realized what was happening—the strife he had caused—and I began to resent him terribly. I wouldn't speak to him, I wouldn't write to him, I wouldn't talk to him on the phone (I lived with my father), and I purposely did things to hurt him. I did things only with my mother and left him out completely.

Now I've come to realize I have to accept him, try to include him, and understand that he probably feels left out sometimes.

There's also a spiritual dimension to the problem, because he's an agnostic. My witness to him is important. Someday I hope I'll have a genuine love for him—and not just for the witness. But it's been hard for me.

I also had a hard time with my dad's second wife. She lived

with us for seven years, then walked out and divorced my dad during my sophomore year in college. She denounced all the things my mother did and then she did the very same thing. She didn't really care about us kids, and to this day we don't speak or write to each other.

I tried to communicate with her. I wrote her long letters afterward, opened myself up to her, and tried to find out if she really cared. Finally I realized that she didn't. I think it's going to be a long time before we are able to talk to each other again—if ever.

Rob: Neither of my parents has remarried, so I haven't had to deal with stepparents yet. But my dad has dated a number of people through the years. It's hard on us kids each time we meet my dad's date. (I live with my mom, but I see my dad quite a bit because we live in the same city.) And what's worse, some of my dad's dates are people my age. It's hard to respect him when I see the poor relationships he's building.

On the other hand, I admire my mom tremendously. She's never dated and never sought another relationship that might lead to marriage. She's really assumed her responsibility for us kids and tried to do the job of both parents. I admire my mom for not putting us in the conflict of a stepfather situation.

Steve: Our family situation was different: all of us kids had either married or gone off to graduate school, and my mother was home alone after my father left. So we encouraged her to remarry if at all possible. She ended up marrying a doctor whom she met in church. He has a strong Christian background, and he's a generous, sharing kind of man. He's been so good for my mother, and also for the rest of the family.

In what ways has your parents' divorce affected your ideas about marriage, relationships, or your image of yourself?

Steve: It has made me cautious with my relationships in a healthy way. People ask me sometimes, "You've only gone out with a couple of people and you've been in college for three years. Why aren't you going out with anyone now?"

I feel that I don't want to make the same mistake my parents did. I know what a monstrous step marriage is. Sometimes it's frightening to see people step into relationships so lightly. Some people have a courtship-and-wedding-day idea of marriage, and they don't realize that marriage is a long haul.

Reflecting on how my father treated my mother has made me want to treat the people I go out with better. Sometimes I go overboard in a dating relationship—that is, developing it so slowly and so cautiously—to the point that it becomes all work and no joy.

Rob: One thing I've seen in my "dating life" is that the other person has to understand my past because my past affects the way I relate to her and vice versa. If the people we date know some facts about our background, they can understand our viewpoints and our behavior better.

Steve: I have found myself looking for the "right" characteristics in people. I don't apologize for that attitude. I'm glad that I'm still unmarried; I'm not quite ready for marriage since the divorce was so recent. Sometimes I see a bit of my father in me. Whenever I do, I get doubly cautious and possibly even hold back more from pursuing relationships with women.

Judy: I was too young to be able to sort out the situation like you did, Steve. I was completely caught up in the divorce. It affected my whole image of myself. I felt emotionally and physically deprived, so my reason for dating was to fill that need. And my dating relationships were very physical. I think a lot of kids are emotionally messed up because of divorce, and may go into marriage even more quickly.

Darlene: For a long, long while after the divorce I had a monkey wrench in my self-image. It took me a long time just to be able to relate to guys comfortably. That didn't happen until college, when I made a lot of Christian friends. For a long time my social life was awkward at home and it was hard for me. Who knows whether those problems stemmed from the divorce or just from being adolescent?

Steve: I've come to learn that singleness is not the desperate

situation I made it out to be before. Not that marriage is a prison, but right now there are lots of things that I could not do and places I could not go if I were married. So I'm viewing my singleness as a gift from God. Through my parents' divorce I'm learning that I don't need to rush into marriage.
Rob: The issue is not whether you're married or single, but whether you're fulfilled; that is, each of us walking the way the Lord leads us, whether into marriage or singleness.
How was your relationship with God affected by the divorce, or what spiritual truths did you feel God taught you through this?
Steve: I became a Christian four months after my parents' divorce. I think the divorce brought me closer to God because all of a sudden the security I felt in my family gave way. I never realized how much I used my family for security until it wasn't there.

Immediately after the divorce, some people in the church I attended saw this insecurity in me and thought I needed the more permanent kind of security that Christ could offer. They talked to me and were willing to share my insecurities. So in a way the divorce helped me to see my need for Christ.

Also, my mom's strength and her love and acceptance of me during the year or two before I became a Christian had a profound impact on my life. She had told me she was a Christian. Her strength was one of the reasons that I was able to come to Christ, because it wasn't something she just talked about, it was something that she lived. She really sacrificed for us.
Rob: My family situation changed when I came to God a number of years after the divorce. For years I had stifled any feelings of love for my family. When I became a Christian, I went back to my family and began to try to heal some of our past hurts. I'm trying to be a member of my family again. That has caused a lot of pain, but in the last four years I've seen a lot of growth in all of us. I think it's largely because I became a Christian.
Darlene: Looking back over my situation, I would say the Lord

really gave me grace for those years that I didn't acknowledge my father. I was a Christian at that time, too, but I had no idea what I'd been doing to him. I thought that since I was a Christian and he wasn't, I was doing the right thing and he was doing the wrong thing by walking away from us little kids.

I see how I could have turned right into a road of bitterness—bitter at the Lord for not letting my father come back home, bitter at my father for remarrying—but I never went that way. I think the Lord gave me grace for those times and protected me.

Judy: The divorce in my family brought about God's larger purposes. Both my mom and dad became Christians afterward. The whole situation was instrumental in my accepting Christ. My need was so great to hear that somebody loved me, that when I heard Jesus really loved me, it was tremendous. When I look over the whole awful situation, I see how God worked in spite of everything.

Rob: I think the way a divorce can bring you closer to God is not through having a superspiritual experience of God showering you with comfort and joy and happiness, but rather that you come in touch with who you are as a person. You really experience your humanity. You're broken up over the problems; your emotions are in upheaval. And out of that experience you see God's strength and love ministering to you as a person and helping you through it. In that way God becomes a lot more real because it's in the context of some difficult down-to-earth problems.

What finally helped you cope with the situation?

Steve: The fact that both my parents are remarried and there's nothing I can do about it. I have to accept it. They've been through a lot of emotional strain, and they need me to be understanding and compassionate.

Judy: I agree with you, Steve, but I found that I wasn't able to view my parents that way when I had so much hurt and bitterness inside. I had to deal with my own hurt first.

Some people are able to admit that the divorce crippled them on the inside, but it took me a long time to realize that the problems I was having in college could be traced back to my parents' divorce eight years earlier. In fact, I didn't realize it on my own; I went to a good Christian psychologist who helped me first to express my feelings about my parents and myself, and then to deal with their cause.

That experience changed my life. It helped me see that God wants me to be a whole person and that I don't have to be crippled emotionally for the rest of my life because my parents got divorced. Now I can feel free to be myself—to communicate better, to express my feelings, and deal with crises as they arise, not months or years later.

Having gone through this experience and grown to a better understanding of myself, I am better equipped to look at my parents, understand their limitations and determine how I can help and be a part of my family.

Rob: You can't deal with your family problem until you've taken care of your own feelings and worked it out within your own self. Otherwise, when you communicate, you do it out of a torn self. But if you've dealt with your own feelings and gotten them out, then you can work toward better communication and understanding with your parents.

Darlene: A big thing that helped me was getting in with a real supportive group of Christian friends at college. They loved me and cared about me, not because I had gone through a divorce, but because we were good friends and they made me feel good about myself.

I can't emphasize enough how devastating my parents' divorce was to my self-image (that is, my feeling of being an O.K. person). It left me feeling that if my own father left me then he must not really have loved me; and if *he* didn't love me then I must be an unlovable, worthless person.

But my friends really liked me, truly loved me, and helped me to see that in God's sight I really *am* worth something—I really am lovable. I can feel good about myself and be confident

in my relationships with others.
What suggestions would you offer to people who are in situations similar to yours?
Steve: I'd say that every situation is going to be different. Nobody can give you a pat answer. We can see that here.
Judy: A divorce affects all areas of your life, but especially the emotional side. I would encourage everybody not to be ashamed to undergo professional counseling, preferably from a psychologist or psychiatrist who's a Christian.
Rob: One thing that helps is to spend time with other people who are having healthy relationships with each other and with God. Then you have something to model yourself on. If all you see is messed-up relationships, then you will probably have a warped perspective on relationships.

I think you'll find yourself doing this unconsciously. Don't be afraid to identify someone as a mother or father image. You need that.
Darlene: That reminds me, Rob, of a missionary couple I stayed with for a few months in Bolivia. I was very impressed by their love for each other and their communication. I saw their problems, too, but I came away with a good perspective of what a marriage could be.

That experience was one of the big turning points in my deciding that I even wanted to be married. For a long time I didn't want to have anything to do with marriage. I had career plans. Then when I started dating, my ideas changed, though I was still cautious. Now I've come around to seeing what a marriage can be and really wanting to get married, if it's the Lord's will.
How important do you think it is to communicate with both of your parents about the divorce and your feelings about it?
Darlene: My father and I have talked about how it's affected us. Once he said to me, "There's not a night that goes by that I don't wonder if there could have been another way out. I've got a lot of regrets about what happened. But it's over now." On the other hand, I don't get in touch with my mom's feelings about it at

all. She doesn't ever let me see those feelings.

If I were a parent getting a divorce, I would definitely talk to my kids about it. When I was young I didn't talk to anybody. When kids came over to my house I'd say, "This is my parents' room." I wouldn't let them know that my parents were divorced because I felt so strange about it. I would encourage parents that are divorced not to make it a hush-hush thing, but to realistically explain the situation and don't be afraid to say, "We're sorry for what happened, but that was the only thing we could do at the time."

Steve: My mother has talked pretty freely about the reasons for her divorce. She sat me down one day and got very basic for two or three hours. It was a relieving, cleansing type of experience. It was good for her, too, because she had some of her feelings bottled up for a long time.

Rob: It was five years before I talked to anyone about the divorce. During that time I went around feeling I was the only person in this situation, when there were people all around. It's so important to talk over your feelings with someone. It would be great if your parents helped you deal with those emotions. Yet in some cases your parents can't or won't do it. Then you've got to find some other understanding people (preferably adults) to talk to instead.

A divorce in your family is not something you go through one day and then forget about. Those feelings will stay with you for the rest of your life. Even if you become a Christian as we did, the scars and hurts of the past don't go away. But you do have a better means of dealing with those hurts when you have Christ in your life. It's not a hopeless situation. It can become better when you deal with it out in the open.

Part 4
Growing Up

Will I Always Be Mama's Baby?

by Lynn Bunch

14

My apartment door stood ajar. My watch said 1:00 A.M. In the eerie light of my desk lamp gleamed a snub-nosed .38 and the sweaty brow of the man who held it.

"Get in here," he ordered.

I stepped inside, clutched by the same numb feeling I used to get in grade school when the loud-speaker summoned me to the principal's office.

"Who are YOU?" I said in a shaky voice. "This is MY apartment!"

"I'm Sergeant Johnson of the Athens City Police," he said calmly. While holding the gun on me, "Sergeant Johnson" claimed that someone had pried off the screen and come in the unlocked window. "One of your neighbors called and I rushed right over," he said, trying hard to sound like a policeman. He whipped out a dimestore badge. "Check and see what's missing."

"My roommate, for starters," I mumbled. Afraid of what I might find, I hurried to see if Michelle was all right. She'd slept through the whole thing. When I came back with Michelle, the intruder shoved the gun in his pocket, but he still held onto it. I talked to him for fifteen minutes, asking him everything I could think to ask a "policeman": Should we get a gun? What size? How old did I have to be? Did I have to register it? And on and on. After cordial thank yous and good-bys, I followed him to his car. I got the license number and called the *real* police.

At 3:00 A.M., while detectives dusted my plant pots and picture frames, my only thought was, "What am I going to tell Mother and Daddy?" I was sure Mother would hop on the next plane and move me right back into the dorm. "I told you to be careful," she'd say. "You just aren't old enough to take care of yourself!"

Declaration of Independence Independence—the Triple Crown, the Wimbledon of growing up?

But at what price? Sometimes it's pretty steep. I thought for a long time that the only way I'd ever be independent was to cut my parents out of my life as much as possible. But this doesn't have to be the case. If you keep the following guidelines in mind as you ease toward independence, you won't have to learn them the hard way.

First, *don't pull.* I decided to go to college as far away from home as possible. I thought unless I showed my parents that I didn't need them to do anything for me, they'd never let me do anything for myself. So I told them about the robbery during Christmas vacation—three months after it happened.

There were other things I kept secret even longer—such as the time I forgot to put on the emergency brake and my car rolled back into me. After I squeezed out from between the wall and my car, I spent the next two weeks on crutches. And when I went to shoot a photojournalism assignment and parked in a muddy ditch, I paid the tow truck in cash.

It took me a long time to learn that a real adult has the guts to be honest. Anybody can be independent by running away from someone else, but it's a different story to be self-reliant and close to others at the same time.

Second, *don't push.* Don't push your values on your parents. If they sense that your love for them depends on whether you like what they do, they will feel pressured and cornered. A dog will bite if you corner it; sometimes parents wish they could do the same.

Colorblind An experience from my freshman year showed me the value in giving my folks room to change.

"What are you trying to do to us?" Mother cried over the phone. "What are you trying to prove?—Abbie's *Black!* Did you think about what Daddy's people in Atlanta will *think?*"

"Honey," my father began. "Of all the girls you know in Athens, why do you *have* to room with *her?*" His quiet voice was strained. I could see him sitting at home in his mechanic's "blues," hurt and misunderstood.

I shifted my seat on the metal air vent in my dorm room as they waited for my answer. The dreadful silence felt like the dark calm during a tornado watch. How could I tell them that I'd had no motive, no point to prove? How could I ever make them see that Abbie became my friend so quickly that I never thought about what color she was? Mother and Daddy were Christians —shouldn't they understand?

"You were the ones who told me that God loves everyone alike!" I sobbed, tears running down my neck and onto my shirt. "How can you tell me I'm wrong to have Abbie as a friend because she's Black?"

Neither of us understood each other. I hung up, hoarse and disillusioned. I knew the worst part would be telling Abbie.

"I can't make you an issue between us," I said to her, embarrassed. "Every time they'd call, you'd feel strange if you answered. I'm sorry. Please don't condemn them. They never had parents to teach them the love they taught me."

"Look," she said smiling. "I do understand." She put her arm around me. "Things like this don't always last forever, Lynn. Don't you judge them either. If you love them through all of this, they'll come around. They wouldn't have told you something if somewhere deep down they didn't believe it themselves."

That spring quarter my sister Gwen suddenly got in a jam for a roommate. Abbie moved in to help her out. I knew the roof would fall in when my parents found out.

"Mother and Daddy called last night," Gwen told me one morning. "They apologized. They even talked to Abbie and thanked her for helping me out. Can you believe it?"

No, I really didn't, I'm sorry to say. For a while I suspected everything they said was a put-on. But it was fourteen-carat, the real thing.

Rose-colored Glasses Finally, *don't preach.* It's easy to condemn someone's prejudice against Blacks or Jews, or get angry at condescending cracks about women. I can't understand how my church turns up its nose at kids in jeans and coddles bankers in five-hundred-dollar suits. And if the missions fund is so deep in the red, why do some of the church leaders drive Mercedes? Yet sometimes my twenty-twenty vision gets blurred when it comes to my own life.

When I was in high school, the Jesus Movement hit like a summer rainstorm. I joined a group with instant answers to worry, sickness, sadness and disappointments. We had some second blessing that suddenly made us mature Christians like Instant Breakfast makes milk a meal. We "rejoiced" over our mountain-top experience and prayed for people (such as our parents) who had never found out what Christianity was all about.

I didn't need insurance, or doctors, or medicine, I decided. God promised that if I believed, I'd never have any problems. If I only prayed hard enough, all the wars and crimes would go away and the world would be perfect. I wasn't fazed when I offended other Christians. I thought it showed how much more Spirit-filled I was. The world wasn't supposed to understand "spiritual things."

God's job was to say yes to my prayers. My idea of worship was some emotional high that soon wore off and didn't change how I acted toward people such as my family.

Parental Consent In spite of the flak they got from the elders and deacons at our church, Mother and Daddy let me go to these meetings. They thought I was trying to find out who God was, and they trusted that I'd eventually get back on track—all on my own. Meanwhile, I kept on praying that they'd get Spirit-filled and I preached to them at breakfast, lunch and supper.

A teacher who sponsored the group kept talking to me about healing. "God wants to heal your eyes so you won't have to wear glasses anymore," she said. "Don't you believe that God doesn't want you to wear glasses? You just need to ask him and then believe that he has healed you, even though you may not be able to tell the difference right away."

I knew she believed it because she drove to school every day without her glasses and thought that God had healed her eyes. To her, healing was a "proof" of spirituality, some top rung on a spiritual ladder. I became convinced that everybody's experience with God could be the same; all I had to do was push the right button and wait.

Father Knows Best Mother almost hit the ceiling. "I pay for you to have glasses and then you refuse to wear them. You look like a fool walking around when you can't see!"

"My only concern is that you get your schoolwork done," Daddy told me. "How can you copy notes from the board? I know you can't see. Why, you can't even recognize people on the street!"

They were right: I *couldn't* see. And when I couldn't see after two weeks, I felt like a fool.

"God didn't fail you," Daddy told me. "You tried to make him an errand boy for whatever you wanted. God doesn't bless you because you do the right combination of things or say the right words. Every gift of God is undeserved. It's grace."

He showed me 2 Corinthians 12:7-10, where Paul talks about his "thorn in the flesh" that God refused to take away. "My grace is sufficient for you, for my power is made perfect in weakness," Paul says. "I will all the more gladly boast of my weaknesses, that the power of Christ may rest upon me . . . for when I am weak, then I am strong." In Philippians 4:11 he adds, "I have learned, in whatsoever state I am, to be content."

That's the danger of preaching to your parents; sometimes it turns out that they were right all along. But even if you don't pull, push or preach to your parents, that doesn't guarantee that the kind of freedom you've got is top value. You need a guide to quality.

When They're Sixty-four Although you've heard 1 Corinthians 13 at almost every wedding you've gone to, Paul wasn't writing to his fiancée. He told us how to measure the love content of relationships. He could have said, "If I become the most self-actualized, independent single person in America, and have not love, *I am nothing.*" This kind of love takes parents' needs into account and faces up to the things we owe them as children. As you read "Love is patient, love is kind . . . love does not insist on its own way," you might say, "Wait a minute. I'll never cut the apron strings this way! I'll always be Mama's baby!"

My mother used to be a nurse. Her idea of being needed was when she could *do* something for somebody—rub someone's back, feed or bathe someone. So when I got out on my own, seven hundred miles away, Mother thought I didn't need her. She couldn't do my laundry or nurse me when I got sick. What was she supposed to do after twenty years when her reason for living flew the coop? It's taken three or four years of sharing the worry over rent, my ruined cakes and casseroles, and the pride of my first embroidery for her to really believe that being needed means a lot more than being a nursemaid. I still need her as a friend.

Paul adds, "But when I became a man, I put away childish things." College years can be great times to "put away childish things." But that doesn't include putting away your parents for the duration. Go to them for advice and counsel when you can. Nurture your relationship. You'll need it for the rest of your life.

Preparing for Marriage

by Jim Conway

15

Many people wonder, "How can I prepare now so I'll start out with a good marriage?"

God has definite intentions for you as you begin this preparation. Genesis 1:26-28 and 2:18-25 spell out patterns that are extremely significant for establishing a good life partnership. We discover that God created man incomplete when he was the only human being in the world. Then God made a suitable person, Eve, who met Adam's created need. God designed people with a need for each other and said this was good (Gen 1:31).

I'd like to suggest five areas of preparation I feel are essential for building a strong foundation for marital life:

1. Be Prepared to Meet Needs.

A primary task of husband and wife is meeting each other's needs; that's what God intends marriage to be. These needs include companionship, shared responsibility in raising children, intimacy and affection. Don't enter into marriage until you understand all the needs of that relationship and are prepared to do all you can to meet them.

Notice also in the Genesis 1 account that God gives the husband and wife shared responsibilities in rulership over the other creatures and the world. There is not one ruler only, but the plural is used repeatedly for the oversight of the creation. In Genesis 3 it is clear that God called Adam accountable for the marriage leadership. This does not teach that males are always to be leading females in every task in the world; rather, a companionship leadership is set forth.

2. Seek Good Counsel.

Preparing for a strong marriage also means involving other people to give you insight. That can come through premarital counseling with a trained pastor or marriage counselor or through marriage seminars. Involve your parents in the procedure of choosing and preparing for marriage. They may see some things which from your point in life you can't see. Other couples who have been married for a time can give you important insights concerning what to look for in a marriage partner and how to make your marriage effective.

Hundreds of books on marriage and relationships are available. Commit yourself to read at least a dozen solid Christian books on topics such as understanding the opposite sex (they *are* different!), handling finances, relating to in-laws, managing sexual needs, choosing careers, rearing children, using leisure time and forming the spiritual life of the family. Take advantage of the accumulated wealth of information that the body of Christ has developed in recent years.

3. Be Realistic.

Many times the choice of a life partner is basically an emotional one. Seek to balance that emotion with a rational understanding of yourself, your needs and potential, and the qualities and needs of the person you want to marry. There are hundreds of areas you should look at as you make a rational choice, to find the person who is best suited for you.

Ask yourself "real life" questions *before* you consider engagement. They are crucial to your understanding of each other —and to whether you should consider engagement. How do you feel about the use of money? What are your career goals? Are they complementary or conflicting? What are your material expectations for the future and what will be required to fulfill them? Do you want to have children? How many and how soon? If you disagree on these or other issues, have you worked out a resolution that is agreeable to both parties? Or do you think you'll change your mate's thinking after you marry?

You love each other, but do you *like* each other? How do you deal with things about the other person that bug you? How do you handle it when your partner criticizes you or expresses dissatisfaction about some aspect of the relationship? Do you make decisions by mutual consensus and prayer, or do you "fall in" to most of them?

Have you discussed divorce and your feelings about it? What will you do if your marriage reaches a point of real crisis? Does one or both of you see divorce as an option at that point?

Talking things through will not kill your affection. It will guarantee that your decision will be a good one. A hard rational look at all aspects of this lifetime partnership you're considering will mean more satisfaction and less disappointment throughout your marriage.

4. Be Honest and Open.

Preparing for a good marriage will demand a great deal of honesty between you and your mate. You need to be sensitive to the slightest movements in each other's personalities. You cannot ignore small signals coming from either of you and say, "Oh well, that's not important."

Imagine yourself hooked up to a polygraph machine. As you talk with each other about these hundreds of items that will make or break your marriage, listen and watch the graph. When the needle jumps, stop and ask yourself why you're uneasy. What needs to be talked out further? Be willing to take the necessary time to honestly work through those areas until you are in agreement.

I have counseled many couples who swept numerous "small" concerns under the rug when they were dating, ignoring the signals. Later, in marriage, these became growing tension points, much like a small stone in a shoe which isn't noticed at first but becomes excruciating after a while.

5. Look to God.

Remember that God is on your side in your marriage preparations. You are not doing this all by yourself. Marriage was God's idea in the first place, and he is more concerned that you have a good marriage than you are! Trust him with this area of your life. Ask him for insight into yourself and other people. Allow him to prepare you to be the person your future mate needs, as well as to prepare your mate for you.

Years before I was married, I prayed regularly for two women, the one I was currently dating and the one who would eventually become my wife. Ultimately I was praying for the same woman. Good marriages are rare, but walking with God and carefully preparing yourself will enable you to experience one of life's greatest joys.

Life's Little Blessings

by Phyllis Le Peau

16

Suddenly all the faces in the room went blank. This group of friends, usually lively, animated, laughing, now sat silent. My husband, Andy, had just told them that we were expecting our third child. We were excited. But their response was silence, then frowns of concern or pity.

We discovered later that their response to the news was not unique. A positive reaction—"I'm delighted!" "Praise God!"—was unusual. Many people couldn't imagine why anyone would want more than two children (especially if you already have one boy and one girl). They feel that children are an inconvenience, a nuisance, an expense. There are too many other things to do, too many places to go. "I will make myself happy." "I must do my own thing." The world has molded negative attitudes toward childbearing and childrearing, and, as in other ways, the church of Jesus Christ has often imitated it.

Yet God says that children are a heritage, a reward. A person who has a quiver full of them will be happy (Ps 127:5). Jesus said, "Whoever receives one such child in my name receives me; but whoever causes one of these little ones who believe in me to sin, it would be better for him to have a great millstone fastened round his neck and to be drowned in the depth of the sea" (Mt 18:5-6). Children are considered gifts. Jacob spoke of his children as being graciously given by God (Gen 33:5). Proverbs speaks of children as "the crown of the aged" (Prov 17:6). In biblical times, being childless was cause for despair. Sarai, Rachel, Hannah and Elizabeth greatly desired children and joyfully praised God when he answered their prayers. What a contrast to today!

Showers of Blessing Andy and I have found God's promise of blessing to be true in five specific areas:

First, *I have learned to appreciate my Creator and his creation more.* The miracle which occurred at the moment our first child was born had a great impact on me. It affected our relationship with God, our Creator and Stephen's Creator. To hear that cry, to know that at one time Stephen did not exist but that now he does, to ponder that he is made in the image of the Almighty God, to receive Stephen as a gift from God to be nurtured and cared for—all of this made us grateful and humble. That awe continued as we watched two more children come into the world. God is indeed a great Creator!

Seeing the world through the eyes of small children also increases my appreciation for the creation. The wonder of a lightning bug, the beauty of a butterfly, the taste of an ice cream cone, the uniqueness of a leaf or a snowflake—all take on new meaning as I see them through the delighted eyes of a child. Susan never takes a walk without bringing home a very special rock. Stephen readily exclaims, "Isn't that a beautiful flower!" Even on his fussiest days, Philip grows content when we go outside.

Second, *my appreciation for God as my Father has grown.* I

know how much I love my children. The affection I feel as I nurse Philip or cuddle Susan or hug Stephen is deep and flows through me like the waves of an ocean. My desire for their well-being is greater than I have felt for almost anyone. The pain I feel when they are hurting is worse than when I hurt myself. I want to protect them. I want to take their pain. I have loved them in ways that I have loved no one else. God says he loves me even more!

"Can a woman forget her own baby and not love the child she bore?" I yell No! "Even if a mother should forget her child, I will never forget you. . . . I have written your name on the palms of my hands" (Is 49:15-16 TEV).

I also know my grief, impatience and anger when my children disobey. I want so much for them to learn obedience because I want them to grow into respectful, responsible individuals. I want them to learn to obey me so that they will learn to obey God.

God grieves when I disobey him. His patience with me stands in stark contrast to my lack of patience with my children. My children and God are teaching me that obedience is not instant and does not last forever. It is learned over a lifetime—and he lovingly waits for me to learn.

Gritting My Teeth Third, *my children have helped me experience the painful happiness of learning about myself.* It is painful to see my sin more clearly. It is happiness because I can confess and change and grow more like Jesus.

What have I learned? That I am inwardly an angry person. My kids can make me angrier than anyone else in the world can. It's hard to admit that about a two-year-old and a four-year-old. I want to shake Susan hard when she looks me straight in the eye and says, "I don't *want* to brush my teeth!" or changes from an angel to a terror as she is told she can't go to work with Daddy. I yell at Stephen when I have told him three times not to play with the hose and he does it again. Sometimes I grit my teeth when eight-month-old Philip refuses to stop fussing when I am trying to get supper on the table and there is a meeting at seven o'clock.

I don't like my anger. God doesn't like it either. He says in James 1:20, "For the anger of man does not work the righteousness of God." But he forgives. And my children are quick to forgive. Experiencing God's forgiveness is as refreshing as a cool shower after mowing the grass on a hot, muggy day.

Living with children has helped me be more "quick to hear, slow to speak, slow to anger" (Jas 1:19). They need time to say what's on their minds. They need to have me listen—not to assume blame and guilt without hearing.

Fourth, *I've learned I am weak and dependent on God.* Does that sound negative? It's not, because God promises that his strength is perfected in my weakness. The more I see my weakness, the more I depend on God for his strength. I need God's strength merely to get up in the morning for my exercise and quiet time. Neither has ever come easily for me. After Philip has interrupted a night's sleep three times, or I'm drained from caring for a sick child, it's even more difficult. I need God's strength to be patient. When it's the third time Susan has wet her pants and Stephen has awakened the baby with his noisy ways (not unlike my own), I respond to them differently with God's help than when I handle it in my own strength. I need God's grace to be a servant. Even serving my children does not come naturally to me. Once a friend said (and she is a marvelous mother), "Raising children is the hardest thing I've ever done. Why, it's harder than living the Christian life!"

Big Boy The final area of special blessing children bring into our lives is *the joy that comes from observing their spiritual, emotional and physical growth while we disciple them.* Andy and I are a goal-oriented couple. We spend a few days each year evaluating the previous year and planning what is to come. Then every few months we re-evaluate and adjust our goals. We are seeking God's priorities for us and trying to live by those. However, we can state in a few words the top priority we have for our children: that they become committed disciples of Jesus Christ.

What a privilege to be intimately involved in the process! The most important way is our example. That is scary, exciting and purifying. It is scary because we are sinners and often fail. It is exciting to see our influence as our children move toward God. It is purifying to know that six little eyes are watching, taking in my every move and being affected by my every attitude. This makes me want to keep my life pure and to confess sin quickly.

Paul wrote to Timothy, "I am reminded of your sincere faith, a faith that dwelt first in your grandmother Lois and your mother Eunice and now, I am sure, dwells in you. . . . Continue in what you have learned and have firmly believed, knowing from whom you learned it and how from childhood you have been acquainted with the sacred writings" (2 Tim 1:5; 3:15). Even though we think of Paul as Timothy's mentor, Timothy's training actually began with godly parents when he was a small child.

There is joy too in observing all the other ways our children mature. One Sunday morning several months ago Stephen burst into our room fully dressed, jumping with excitement and eyes beaming with pride. "Stephen," we exclaimed, "you dressed yourself!"

He replied, "I've already had breakfast too and I fixed breakfast for Susan!" After we talked over the great accomplishments of the morning he said, "I feel like a big boy!" There was other evidence that Stephen was indeed a big boy! He was taking initiative in picking up toys, cleaning up the yard and clearing the table.

Objections Overruled Now you may be saying, "All you have said is fine, but what about bringing children into a world like ours?" Andy and I have wept as we have considered what could happen to our children because of the kind of world we live in. The effects of sin can be seen everywhere—war, hunger, divorce, pollution. Every generation has had its own myopia—thinking its world the worst (or perhaps the best). Yet even if ours is the worst, does it mean the people of God should pull out? Of all people, Christians should be raising children, demonstrating God's love and character through stable homes, and teaching young ones to be salt and light in a needy world.

Only God knows what the future holds. He does not forget or lose control as he leads you and your children. My parents were not too excited about the world they brought me into, but I'm glad they did. And they are too (I think!).

Another question that arises is, "What if our children don't follow the Lord?" True, there is no guarantee that they will. Nothing would be harder for me than if one of our children decided not to follow Christ. But if that happens, I will not suffer anything that God hasn't already endured. His own children have turned their backs on him. Yet knowing they would do this, he created them, loved them and gave himself for them. We will lead our children, teach them and pray for them, but there will be a time when they can choose to go their own way.

No Elbow Room And what about the question your economics prof is asking: "Doesn't the world have too many people already? North Americans consume too much as it is."

Andy and I have asked ourselves, "Is it right to have more children and add to this problem?" North Americans overconsume whether or not they have children. So we have chosen to have children and live a simpler life. To have no children does not necessarily mean we will consume less. In fact, with two regular salaries in a marriage, we would tend to buy more, save more, invest more, get more and consume more. Much sacrifice can be made with or without children in order to share with a hungry, needy world. The real issue is whether we are willing to sacrifice, not whether we have children. Self-centeredness does not disappear with the choice to be childless.

Many children born into this overpopulated world need homes. More Christian couples should consider adopting some of them. For those who are genuinely concerned about too many people in the world, adoption is a viable plan of action. Andy and I talked about this even before we got married and we are still seriously considering it.

Perhaps you desire to have children but it is biologically impossible. The blessings that come with children are not reserved for those who have natural children. Adopted children can bring the same happiness. Many minority, biracial and international children desperately need homes, parents and love. Older children or children with handicaps are just waiting for parents. The price is great. The neighbors may not accept our bringing such a child into our family. It will cost a great bit of money to get an international child. Family and relatives may react negatively. But the rewards are great too. Friends of ours have a nine-year-old son they adopted when he was two. David had many problems in speaking, relating to people and trusting, because he had been abused before being adopted. The transformation which has taken place in that child since being in a loving home has been wonderful.

There may be other reasons you cannot have children. You may be single. You may have a handicap that would make raising a child difficult. Yet there are other alternatives. Many parents all around you would be more than willing to lend their children for an hour, a day or a weekend. Teach a Sunday-school class. Get involved with families. Invite them over. Invite yourself over to their place. Set a goal of talking to and getting to know one child. Instead of a great big bother or interruption, I think you'll find a bundle of delight and a fresh perspective on life and the world.

One very real danger in not being exposed to children on a regular basis is developing wrong attitudes toward children—"Children should be seen and not heard," or "What a nuisance they are," or "All they do is interrupt." Jesus publicly reprimanded the disciples for not wanting to be bothered with children. However you choose to do it, avoid the sinful attitudes toward a child which harm you and that child, and displease Jesus.

The Virtues of Oatmeal Finally, you may object, "We already have a simple lifestyle. What if we can't afford to raise children? Or what if children would interfere with our careers?" My first response is that we are rich. No matter what our earthly possessions, we are rich. Even the poor in North America are rich compared with some parts of the world.

Second, we are rich in faith and in our relationship with God. We serve a God who has promised to meet our every need. Andy and I have found it exciting to see God miraculously provide for the big things, like Philip's unexpected hospital bills, and the small ones, such as finding a Big Wheel at a garage sale.

Third, children do not need to be given everything they want. In fact, they should not be given it. My parents had financial needs the whole time they raised us. Often we would eat oatmeal for supper because we did not have money for other groceries. To this day my sister laughs and says "Uh-oh, we're in a bad way" when she sees oatmeal on the table.

As a result, I found satisfaction in nonmaterial things. I learned to appreciate deeply what we did have. As I went to college and was involved with other young adults, I found that those who had been raised with a new wardrobe every season found it difficult to be content with what they had. I learned the value of money and how to use it wisely. My parents' love and care, and their grateful spirit and appreciation for people, helped me appreciate such nonmaterial things as family picnics and my relationship with God. I'm glad I did not have everything while I was growing up. We want to raise our children in the same way. And we are learning to trust God to meet our needs.

Larger Christian families have often produced the kind of godly persons we want our children to be. Because they have had few material goods, there is generous sharing and unique caring between family members. We know a family where six kids were raised in a tiny house with very little money. The parents were in the ministry. Now that the children are grown, though they are spread throughout the country, when one breaks up with a boyfriend or breaks an arm, loses a job or has a fire, each sibling will be in touch to help. They seem to know what is important. Their relationship with God is personal and real because they have had to depend on him. Their prayer life is meaningful. Christians who have too much can grow unconsciously independent of God, because they feel so self-sufficient.

Careers on the Altar To say that sacrifice is not involved in raising children would be a gross understatement. There is great sacrifice in raising kids—sacrifice of time, money, energy and even of friendships and relationships. When a married couple decides to place God first, each other second and children third, they place career concerns far down the list. That can be a great sacrifice in our culture, because raising children must be a team effort.

In our case, Andy and I have chosen for me to stay at home with the children. I love being a nurse so it could appear that the sacrifice is mine. But Andy sacrifices too. When he could work late at the office and get ahead, or spend time alone or watch the news after a long day at work, he is more likely to bathe the children, wash the dishes or listen to a weary wife. We do not have a very strict woman's work/man's work division of labor at our home. In fact, I tease Andy that it is his fault that I want more children. He is such a good team member.

This is not the only way to manage a household. There are househusbands who do a super job of running the household and caring for the children while the wife pursues her career. Or both can work part-time and engineer the household part-time. There is always the option of resuming a career after the children are grown. Whatever route you choose, both partners will make career sacrifices. It is important that one person take charge of the household. Too many homes are like hotels—family members going their own ways with no one around to make home the haven it should be.

I'm biased toward having children—lots of them. I believe it is biblical and pleasing to God. Special blessings come with children. My goal is not to talk you into having a lot of children, or even one. But do consider that God might want you to have children. Be certain that it is not the world that is making the decision for you.

Phyllis Le Peau, formerly a staff member of Nurses Christian Fellowship, is coauthor of the Bible study guides Just Living by Faith, Faith That Works *and* One Plus One Equals One.

For Further Reading

How Do You Say, "I Love You"?
Judson J. Swihart helps readers unravel the complexities of saying and hearing "I love you" through a discussion of eight different languages of love. Though addressed primarily to married couples, it also can foster communication between parents and their children. *paper, 96 pages.*

All I Need Is Love
Nancy Anne Smith recounts how a Christian psychologist helped her overcome severe emotional problems caused by a childhood full of cruelty and abuse. Originally entitled *Winter Past. paper, 120 pages.*

Who Needs the Family?
O. R. Johnston, a Christian sociologist, discusses the recent breakdown of the family and presents a theologically informed analysis of marriage, motherhood and fatherhood. *paper, 152 pages.*

Divorce
John R. W. Stott outlines the biblical view of divorce and answers questions that have troubled Christians for centuries. *paper, 31 pages.*

Parents in Pain
John White offers comfort and counsel to parents of children with severe problems: alcoholism, rebellion, homosexuality and even suicide. *paper, 245 pages; study guide, paper, 12 studies.*

Learning to Be a Man/Learning to Be a Woman
Kenneth and Floy Smith have prepared these Bible study guides to help individuals and groups grasp the essence of true masculinity and femininity. *paper, 19 studies each.*

Two into One
Joyce Huggett helps newlyweds and those considering marriage to achieve the God-centered, joyful union marriage was meant to be. Topics include commitment, intimacy, communication and children. *paper, 128 pages.*

First Things First
Frederick Catherwood, reflecting on the Ten Commandments, discusses the practice of biblical ethics in the context of the decay of modern society. *paper, 160 pages.*

Out of the Saltshaker
Rebecca M. Pippert writes a basic guide to evangelism as a natural way of life, emphasizing the pattern set by Jesus. *paper, 192 pages; study guide, paper, 12 studies.*